THE RHYTHM BIBLE

For Students & Professionals who want to gain the ability to sight-sing and play rhythms, from the simplest to the most complex syncopations.

For the first time in print, syncopations are explained, illustrated and classified.

INCLUDES OVER **1,000** EXAMPLES OF RHYTHMIC FIGURES BASED ON JAZZ, ROCK, BLUES, SWING, LATIN, FUNK, BOOGALOO AND OTHER RHYTHMS.

DAN FOX

The author wishes to thank Link Harnsberger and Bruce Goldes for their expertise, and especially Morty Manus for his care and apparently inexhaustible patience.

Drumset, Trumpet, Clarinet, Saxophone, Flute and Marimba courtesy of Yamaha Corporation of America.

Hollow body guitar courtesy of Gibson Guitar Corp.

Microphone courtesy of Neumann USA.

Solid body electric guitar courtesy of Fender Musical Instruments, Inc.

Violin courtesy of Scherl & Roth/United Musical Instruments U.S.A., Inc.

Who this Book is For

The Rhythm Bible may be used to advantage by all students and professionals:

> Singers, Keyboard, Guitar, Bass, Woodwind, Brass and
> String players, Mallet players (Vibes, Marimba, Xylophone)
> and other Percussionists.

Whether you're a student or a professional, performing today's music can be a real challenge. Most instruction books do not adequately prepare musicians to play complex rhythms, especially syncopation. *The Rhythm Bible* was written to help remedy this deficiency. It includes well over a thousand examples of rhythmic figures (based on everything from simple quarter and eighth notes to the most complex syncopations) common in jazz, rock, Latin, blues, funk and other styles. And, for the first time in print, syncopations are explained, illustrated and classified.

Vocalists and instrumentalists who make a thorough study of *The Rhythm Bible* will gain the ability to sing and play difficult syncopations and other complex rhythms at sight.

The Rhythm Bible is organized by complexity of rhythm, from the easiest to the most difficult. It is advisable to start at the beginning and play through the book sequentially. However, if certain rhythms are particularly troublesome, you can start at the section that deals with them.

Part One — Basic Rhythms (pages 11–39)
Part One starts with the simplest rhythms in 4/4 time. It also explores areas that give even experienced players trouble, such as long held notes followed by rapid notes, starting a measure with a rest, and ties over the barline. Eighth-note, quarter-note, and half-note triplets plus their variations are introduced as well as various combinations of 16th notes.

Part Two — Single Syncopation (pages 40–87)
After a brief history and explanation of syncopation (pages 40–41), there are many exercises illustrating the most common one, the anticipated 3rd beat of the measure (pages 42–60). The book next illustrates the anticipated 2nd beat (pages 61–69), anticipated 4th beat (pages 70–79), and anticipated 1st beat (pages 80–87).

Part Three — Double, Triple and Quadruple Syncopations (pages 88–101)
In 4/4 time, you can have as many as four anticipations per measure. This section starts with two syncopations per measure and gradually works its way up to four. And don't miss the interesting discussion "Syncopation and Latin-American Music" on page 90.

Part Four — Syncopated Accents (page 104), Syncopations in Cut-Time (pages 105–106), Double-Time Syncopations in 2/4 and 4/4 (pages 107–113)
Off-beat accents, while not actually syncopations, produce a similar effect. Syncopated figures in cut-time (common in marches, show tunes and Dixieland jazz) and double-time (often found in rock and disco styles) are also included in this section.

Part Five — Basic Rhythms and Syncopations in 3/4 Time (pages 114–121)
The first four sections of this book are devoted to 4/4 time, the meter in which most popular styles are written. This section introduces 3/4 time, first without, then with, syncopations. Hemiolas are also discussed and illustrated.

Part Six — Rhythms in Other Meters (pages 122–129)
Other meters such as 3/8, 6/8, 9/8 and 12/8 are illustrated (pages 123–127). Irregular meters are also discussed and there are two pages of examples in 5/4.

Contents

Suggestions for Practicing

Vocalists can practice this book several different ways:

1. **Tap** the beat with your hand or foot and **sing** the rhythms on "ta," "da" (pronounced "tah" or "dah") or other syllable.

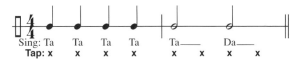

2. **Conduct** the beat with your hand and **sing** the rhythms on "ta," "da" or other syllable.

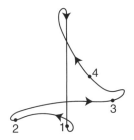

   Conducting will help you keep track of where you are in the measure.

3. **Use a metronome** (preferably an electronic metronome) to keep the beat and **sing** the rhythms as above. Electronic metronomes can be set to mark each downbeat with a louder click so you can keep track of where you are in the measure.

4. **Use rhythm syllables** to sing the rhythms accurately. Rhythm syllables are nonsense syllables similar to those used by scat singers like Ella Fitzgerald or Mel Tormé. Here are our suggestions:

   • For every quarter note, sing "Da." The capital "D" indicates a slight stress or accent.

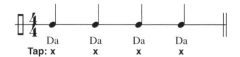

   • The half note is like a quarter note with the "ah" sound extended by one beat.

   • The dotted half note gets three beats.

   • The whole note gets four beats.

How to Use the CD

The CD in the Book & CD kit includes at least one exercise from each music page. These selected exercises are indicated in the book with a CD logo and a track number just above each exercise. They are typical of the rhythms on that page and will be useful in understanding and mastering those rhythms. Some rhythms are recorded in both a straight and swing feel. When that occurs, both will be on the same track, one after the other. Beginning on page 104, examples on facing pages are combined onto the same track.

Each silent beat (or rest) is represented by the unpronounceable syllable "Dp," a click of the tongue or tap of the foot. It is just as important to mark every silent beat as it is to sing the notes.

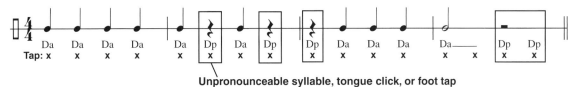

Unpronounceable syllable, tongue click, or foot tap

- Pairs of eighth notes are sung as "Da-ba." The lower case "b" indicates that the upbeat eighth note is stressed less than the downbeat eighth note.

- For eighth note triplets sing "Da-na-va," making sure to keep all syllables the same length.

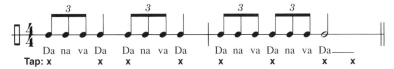

- Groups of four 16th notes are sung as "Da-la-ba-ma," like "Alabama" but with a "D." Notice that the downbeat syllables "Da" and the upbeat syllable "ba" are indicated at the same places in the beat as eighth notes.

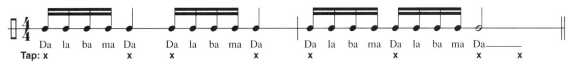

- Sometimes it's useful to write in a syllable to be imagined, not sung, as when playing the dotted quarter/eighth note rhythm. These appear in parentheses.

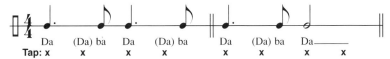

Rhythm syllables are particularly useful when singing syncopations. In the following syncopated figure, the capital letter "B" below the fourth note shows that this note must be accented.

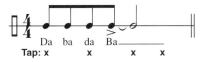

Other syllables can be figured out later in the book. If you find this technique useful, write in rhythm syllables wherever you're having trouble singing a figure accurately. If you don't find them useful, use your own system. What counts is being able to sing the rhythms accurately, so use what works for you. Also, try singing the rhythms using scale tones or improvising in the key of the scale.

Brass, Woodwind, Guitar and Bass Players can practice like this:

1. **Tap** the beat with your foot and **sing** the rhythms on "ta," "da" or other syllable.

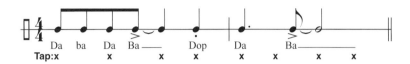

2. **Tap** the beat with your foot and **play** the rhythms on your instrument.
   Stay on one note.

3. **Tap** the beat with your foot and **play** the rhythms on a scale
   or simple chord (major, minor, seventh).

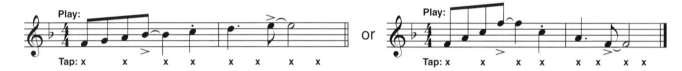

4. **Tap** the beat with your foot and **play** a short, improvised melodic figure
   based on the rhythm.

Note: If you have a **metronome** (preferably an electronic one), set it to accent the downbeat in whatever meter you choose and practice the four steps described above, using the metronome instead of the foot taps.

Pianists and Mallet Players (Vibes, Marimba, Xylophone, etc.) can practice like this:

1. **Tap** the beat with your foot and **sing** the rhythms on "ta," "da" or other syllable.

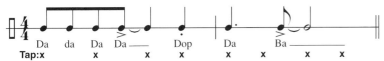

2. **Tap** the beat with your foot and **play** the rhythms on your instrument. Stay on one note.

3. **Left hand plays** the beat on the root tone. **Right hand plays** the rhythm on any note that sounds good with the keynote, for example, the root, third or fifth of the key.

4. **Left hand plays** the beat on the root tone.
   Right hand plays the rhythm on the scale of the key or a simple chord (major, minor, seventh).

 or

5. **Left hand plays** the beat as a moving or stationary line.
   Right hand plays a short melodic figure improvised on the rhythm.

Note: If you have a **metronome** (preferably an electronic one), set it to accent the downbeat in whatever meter you choose and practice the five steps described above, using the metronome instead of the foot taps.

String Players can practice like this:

1. **Tap** the beat with your foot and **sing** the rhythms on "ta," "da" or other syllable.

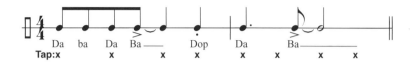

2. **Tap** the beat with your foot and **play** the rhythms on your instrument. Stay on one note.

3. **Tap** the beat with your foot and and **play** the rhythms on a scale:

or simple chord (major, minor, seventh):

4. **Tap** the beat with your foot and **play** a short, improvised melodic figure based on the rhythm

Note: If you have a **metronome** (preferably an electronic one), set it to accent the down-beat in whatever meter you choose and practice the four steps described above, using the metronome instead of the foot taps.

Drummers can practice like this:

1. **Tap** the beat with your foot and **sing** the rhythms on "ta," "da" or other syllable.

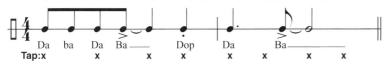

2. **Left hand plays** the beat on the snare drum.
   Right hand plays the rhythm on the cymbal or other drum.

3. **Right or left foot plays** the beat on the bass drum.
   Right or left hand plays the rhythm on the snare drum, cymbal or other drum.

Note: If you have a **metronome** (preferably an electronic one), set it to accent the downbeat in whatever meter you choose and practice the three steps described above, using the metronome instead of the foot taps.

Other Percussionists can practice like this:

1. **Tap** the beat with your foot and **sing** the rhythms on "ta," "da" or other syllable.

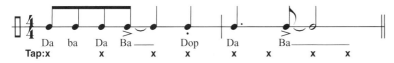

2. **Tap** the beat with your foot and **play** the rhythms on your instrument.

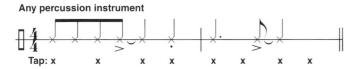

Note: If you have a **metronome** (preferably an electronic one), set it to accent the downbeat in whatever meter you choose and practice the two steps described above, using the metronome instead of the foot taps.

Using a metronome will be a great help in mastering this book. The electronic type of metronome is fairly inexpensive and can be adjusted to mark the first beat of every measure. This is especially helpful when dealing with long notes and rests, as in Ex. 1 (page 12).

Metronome: Tap tap tap tap Tap tap tap tap Tap tap tap tap Tap tap tap tap

Straight vs. Swing Eighth Notes

Straight eighths are eighth notes played mathematically correct, each as long as the others. This is the way they are played in classical, Latin (except for salsa) and rock music. Traditionally, musicians have counted them as "1 & 2 & 3 & 4 &."

Swing eighths are played in groups of two with the first eighth note a little longer and the second eighth note a little shorter than normal. This rhythm is cumbersome to notate accurately, but careful listening to jazz and/or certain types of country will help you internalize the feel. It may be helpful to think of the syllables "da-ba da-ba" to help obtain the correct feel:

Swing eighths

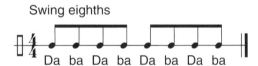

Da ba Da ba Da ba Da ba

Tempo

Set your metronome at a moderate tempo, about ♩=96. Sing or play through each exercise on a page, one at a time, until you can do a complete page of 10 exercises without a mistake or hesitation. Then, sing or play through the 10 exercises without stopping. Mark the tempo at which you can do this perfectly. The next day, set the metronome a little faster, around ♩=100, and sing through all the exercises again. If you can do them flawlessly at the new tempo, mark that tempo and return to the exercises again the next day. Continue in this fashion until you can do the 4/4 exercises at ♩=208 or faster.

Cut time figures should start at ♩=80 and progress to ♩=160 or faster.

For double time figures, start at ♩=52 and progress to about ♩=92 or faster.

For waltzes and other 3/4 pieces, start at ♩=80 and work your way up to ♩.=72 or faster.

For 3/8, 6/8, 9/8 and 12/8, start at ♪=80 and work up to ♩=96 or faster.

It's important to remember, however, that it's better to sing a rhythm accurately and with confidence and authority at a slower tempo, than to use a faster tempo and sound like you're hanging on by your fingernails! Practice slowly. Speed will come in time.

Finally, incorporate whatever rhythms you've been learning into your playing or scat singing. Make up your own figures using the rhythms you've learned, and play them in different keys and on various scales and chords. In this way, you'll not only develop your ability to sight read, but you'll also expand your horizons as far as composing and improvising are concerned.

To Tap or Not to Tap
Is it a good idea to tap your foot constantly? This writer believes not, as the fraction of a second that it takes for the nerve impulse to travel from your foot to your brain can have the effect of making you play behind the beat. It is better to internalize the beat, that is, to hear it within your mind. However, it must be added that many fine musicians disagree, so you must judge by the results you get. When using this book, decide how you will mark missing beats/rests and tied notes. A foot tap or click of the tongue or even a grunt are three possibilities.

PART ONE : *Basic Rhythms*

This book begins with basic rhythms, the familiar whole, half, quarter and eighth notes and rests typical of 4/4 time. These form the rhythmic foundation of all types of music, and we urge you to practice them even if you are already an experienced player. A firm grasp of basic rhythms will help you master the more complex syncopations that follow.

When long notes are held over the bar line, it is helpful to mark the downbeat of the new measure with a foot tap or click of the tongue. This will help you keep track of the downbeats when playing exercises such as Exercises 11–20 (page 13).

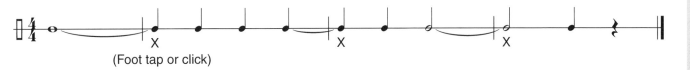

(Foot tap or click)

Another common problem can occur when starting a measure with a rest. We suggest marking the initial rest with a foot tap or click of the tongue. Here again, the metronome will help you keep track of the downbeats.

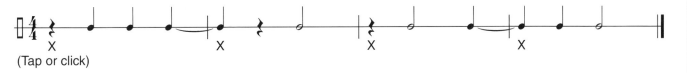

(Tap or click)

Exercise 31 (page 15) introduces eighth notes. Please reread our previous comments (page 10) about the difference between jazz, or swing, eighth notes (long short) and the exactly even, or "straight," eighth notes of other types of music. For swing eighth notes, you can say "da ba da ba." Straight eighths can be counted "1 & 2 & 3 & 4 &."

Also, please be sure to read the introductory material at the top of each page. It will help you with the proper interpretation of each exercise.

Whole, Half & Quarter Notes with Rests

Exercises
1–10

If you find it helpful, foot-tap or tongue-click for every beat of held notes and rests. This is especially important when the notes or rests are held for many beats, such as in Ex. 1. If you wish, you can say "ta," or "da" for each note.

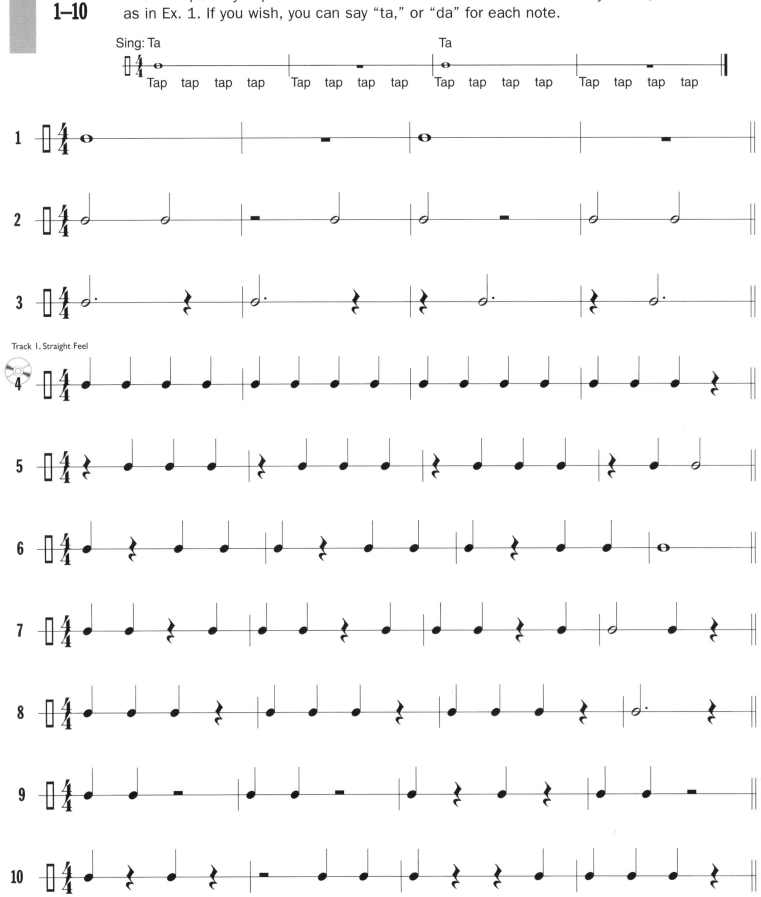

Track 1, Straight Feel

Ties Over the Barline

Exercises
11–20

It is very important to mark rests and tied notes with a foot tap or tongue click.

Make sure you can play this page flawlessly before going on. In Ex. 17 you'll notice two quarters tied in the middle of the measure. This rhythm is often written as a half note. Either way is correct.

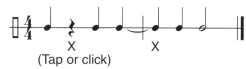

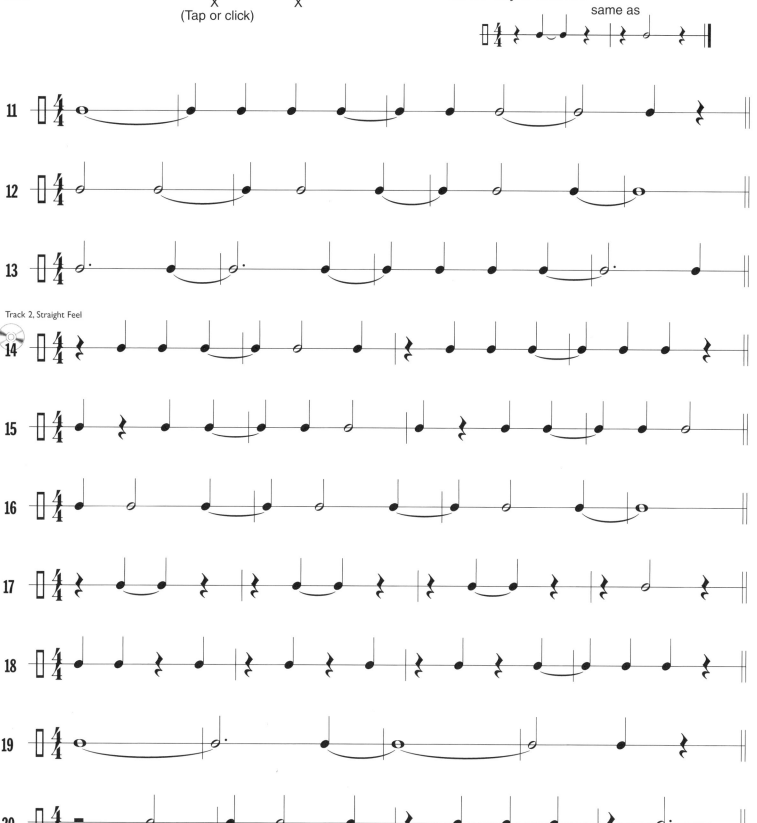

Staccato Dot

Exercises
21–30

The staccato (sta-CAH-to) dot is placed below the note head when the stem goes up, and above the note head when the stem goes down. It means to cut the note short; the remaining part of its time is replaced by silence. If you've been saying "da" for each quarter note, a staccato quarter would be "dop."

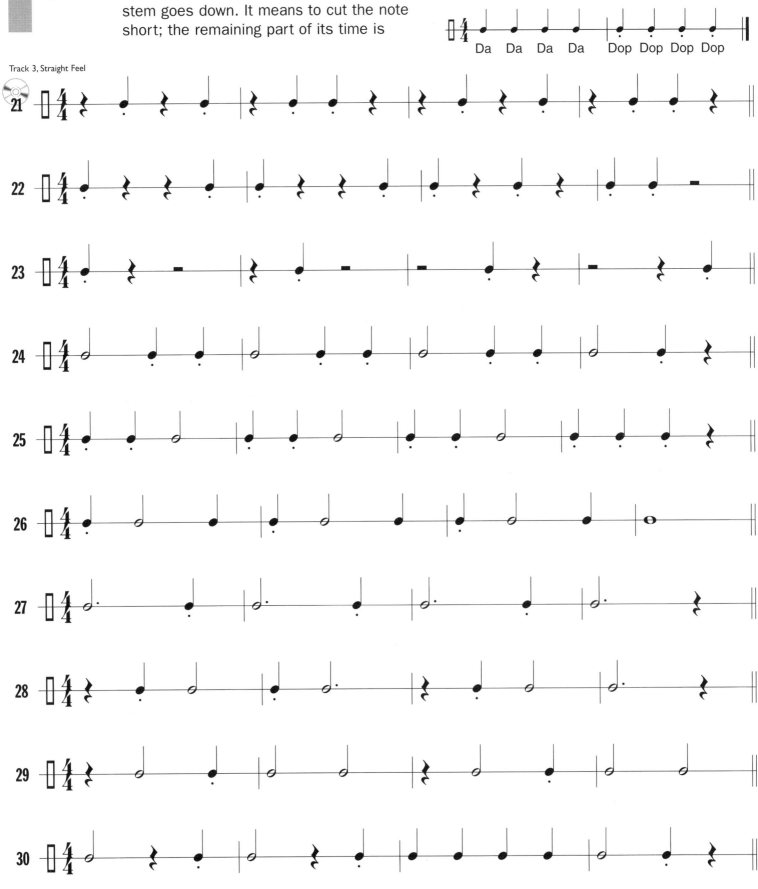

Track 3, Straight Feel

Eighth Notes

Exercises **31–40**

This page introduces eighth notes. Practice the page both with straight eighths ("1 & 2 &") and with swing eighths ("da ba da ba").

Track 4.1, Straight Feel
Track 4.2, Swing Feel

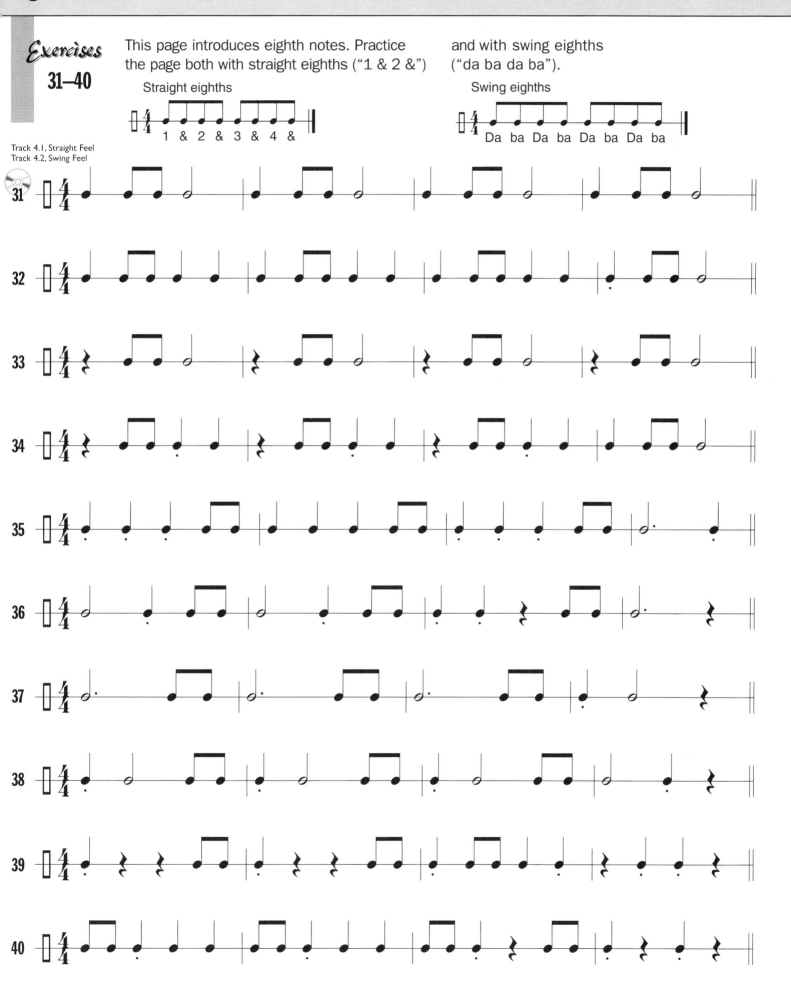

Eighth Notes (cont.)

Exercises
41–50

These exercises combine eighth notes with staccato notes and figures that start with a rest. As always, it is crucial to tap or click for initial rests. Practice both with a straight feel.

and with a swing feel.

Track 5.1, Straight Feel
Track 5.2, Swing Feel

Eighth Notes (cont.)

Exercises
51–60

Here are more combinations of eighth notes, quarter notes, half notes and various rests. When you can play this page flawlessly at ♩=96, gradually increase the speed to 208 or even faster. Don't forget to practice with both a straight and swing feel.

Track 6.1, Straight Feel
Track 6.2, Swing Feel

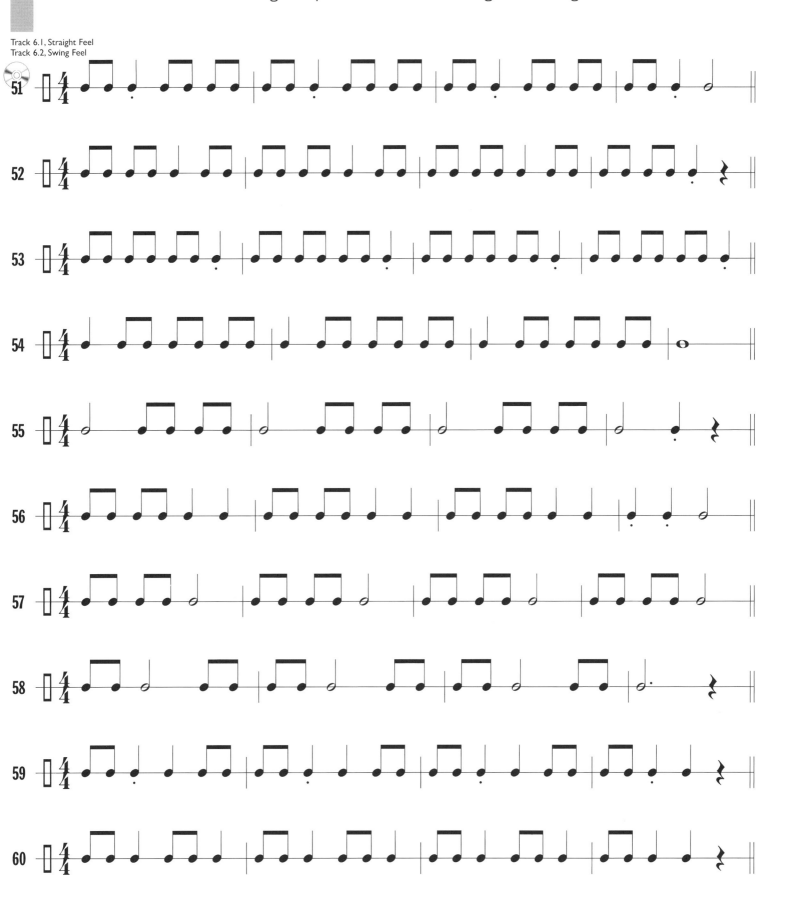

Eighth Notes & Ties

Exercises 61–70

Notes tied across the bar line are often troublesome. Always mark the tied note with a tap or click.

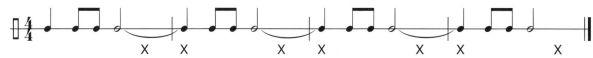

Exercise 70 deals with the problem of following a very long note with shorter notes. Be sure to play this exercise accurately, careful not to rush or drag the eighth notes.

Track 7.1, Straight Feel
Track 7.2, Swing Feel

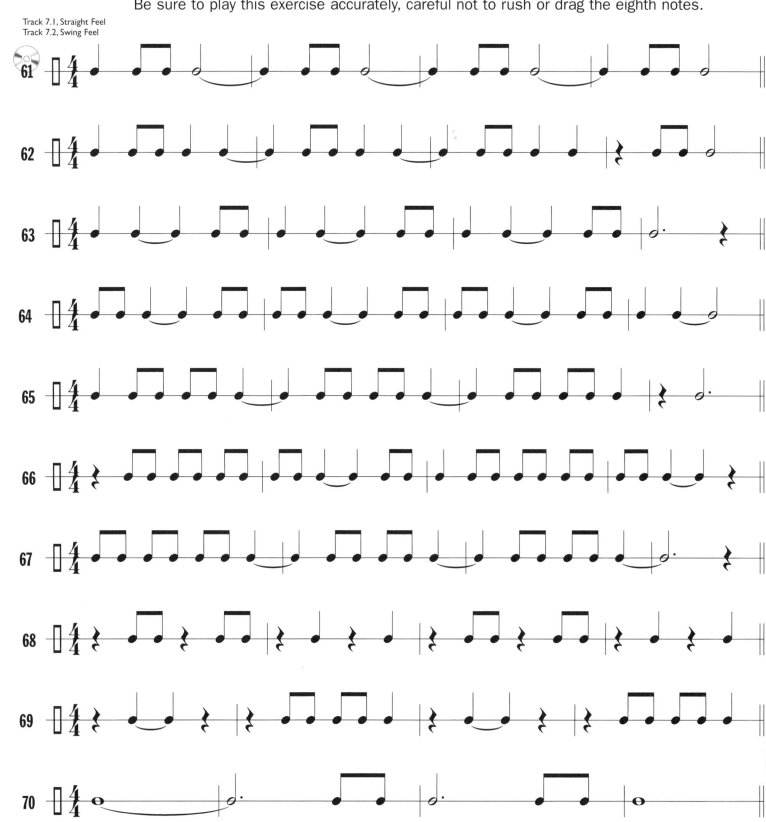

Eighth Notes & Eighth Rests

Exercises
71–80

These exercises introduce the eighth rest. Practically speaking, an eighth note followed by an eighth rest sounds much like a quarter note with a staccato dot. You can say "tut" or "dop" for either rhythm.

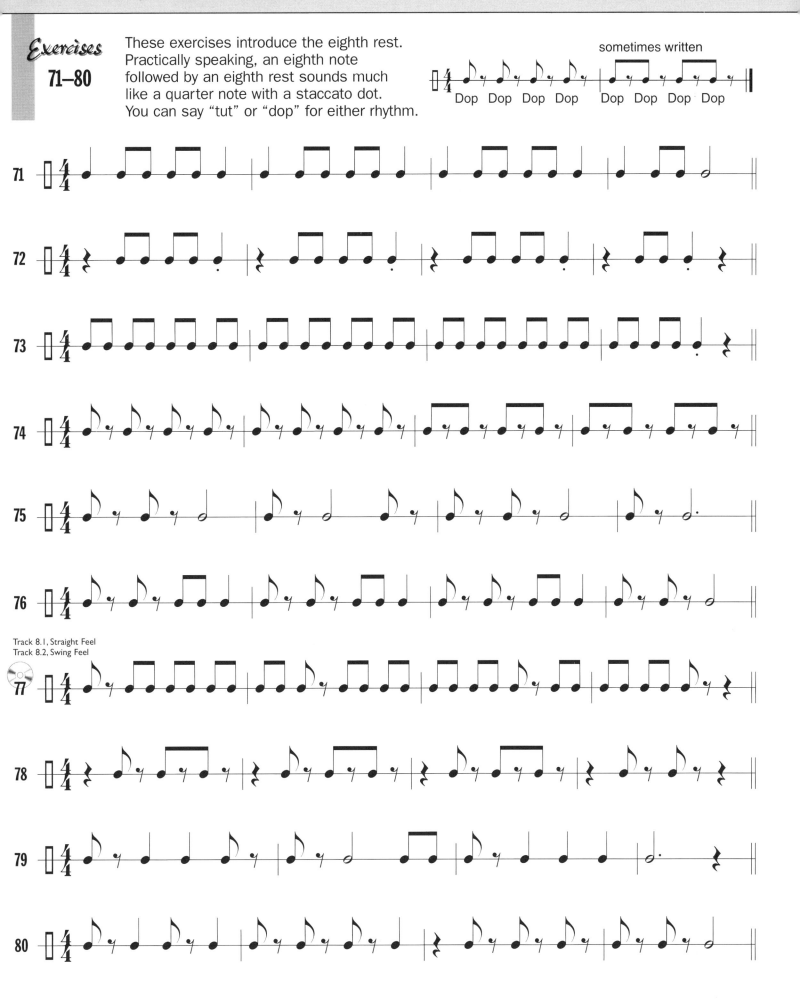

Dotted Quarters & Eighths

Exercises **81–90**

Adding a dot to a note increases its value by half. A dotted quarter note is the same as a quarter note plus an eighth note.

Playing a dotted quarter is simple if the second beat is marked with a foot tap or tongue click.

For swing rhythms try saying "Da (foot tap) ba." For a straight feel, count "1 & 2 &." Make sure the eighth note flows smoothly into the next note.

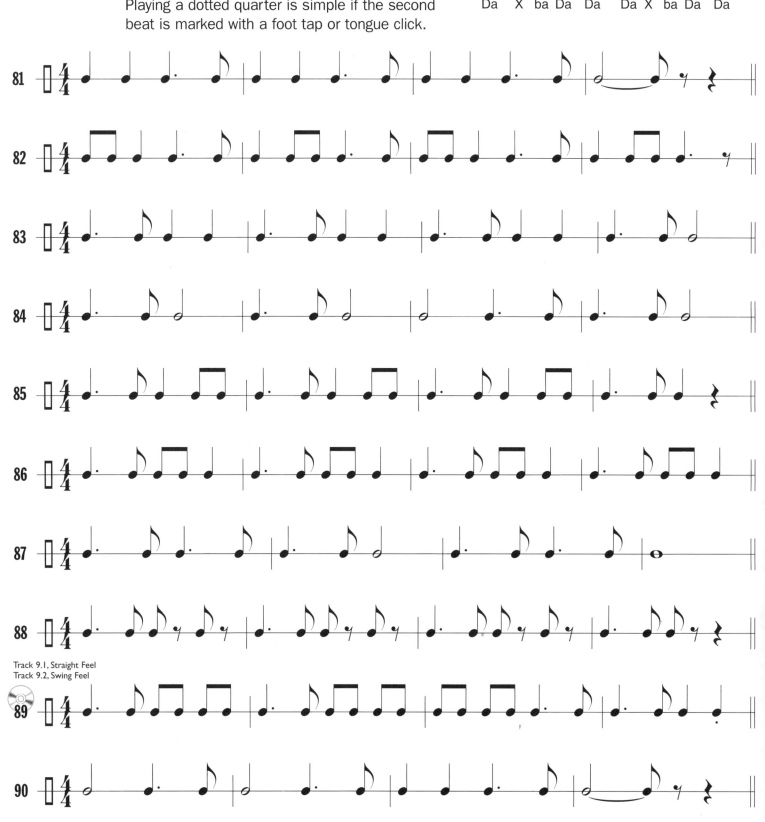

Track 9.1, Straight Feel
Track 9.2, Swing Feel

Eighth Note Triplets *&* Eighth Notes

Exercises 91–100

Work hard to make each triplet flow smoothly into the next note. Use the metronome to avoid the common tendency to rush. In Exercises 96 through 100, contrast the triplets with the eighth notes. If you wish to sing the triplets use, "da-na-va" for a swing feel.

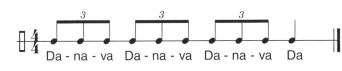

For a straight feel, count "1-trip-let, 2-trip-let," etc.

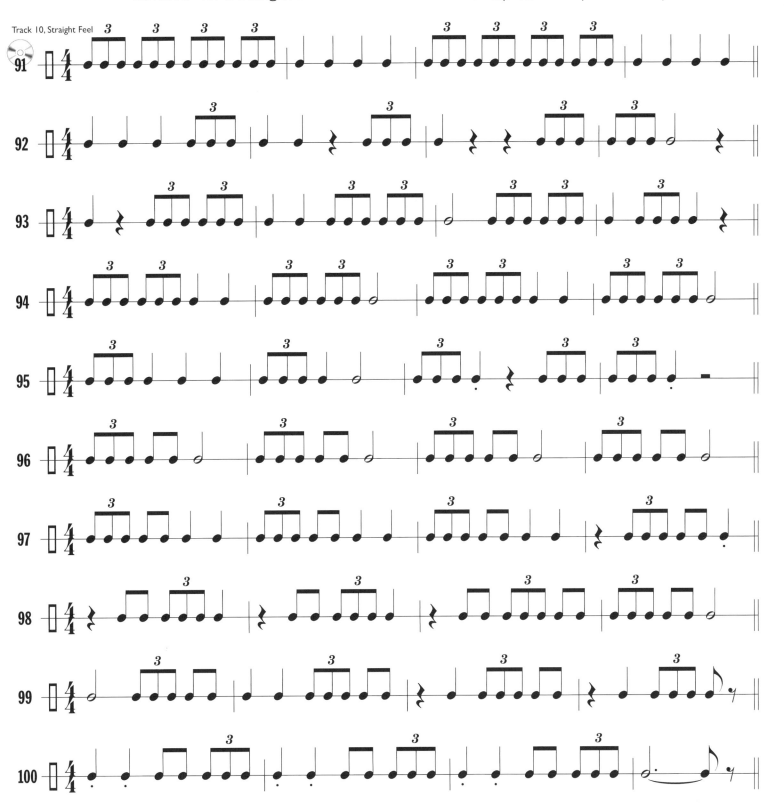

16th Notes in Groups of Four

Exercises
101-110

One of the trickiest things to do rhythmically is contrast fast notes (like 16th notes) and much slower notes (like half or whole notes). Make good use of your metronome when playing this page. If you wish to sing 16th notes, you can use "Da-la-ba-ma" or "tuck-a tuck-a." For straight 16th notes, count "1-uh-&-uh."

Track 11, Straight Feel

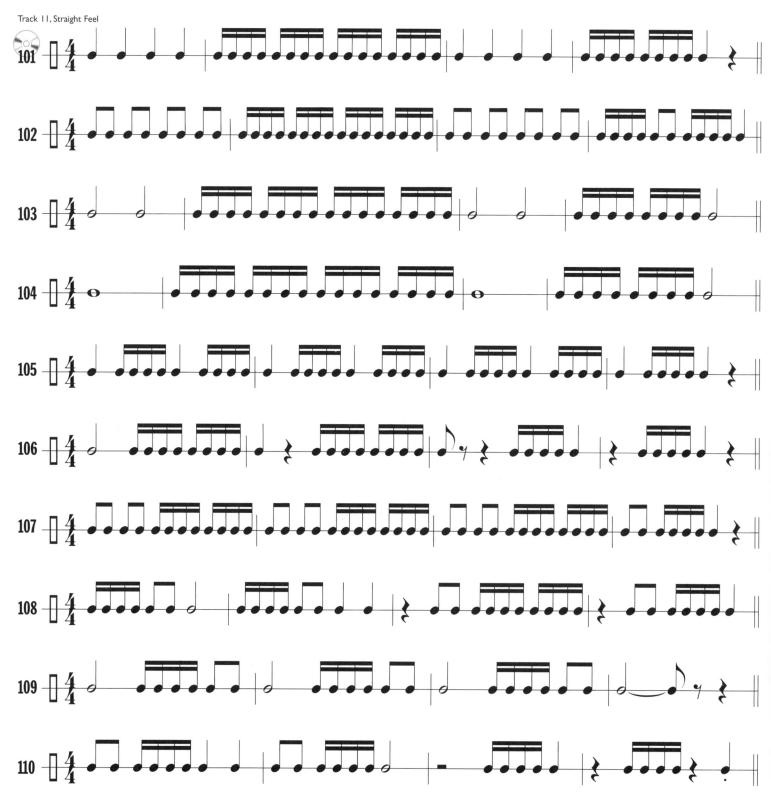

Eighth & Two 16th Note Figure

Exercises 111–120

This very important page deals with the eighth note followed by two 16ths. For straight rhythms, say "1 &-a 2 &-a." Or, say "Rott-weil-er, Rott-weil-er" or "Da-ba-ma, Da-ba-ma."

Track 12, Straight Feel

Two 16th Note & Eighth Note Figure

Exercises
121–130

These exercises are rhythmically the reverse of those on page 23. You can count "1-uh-&, 2-uh-&," or, say "but-ter-milk, but-ter-milk" or "Da-la-bam, Da-la-bam." Be especially careful when the basic figure is contrasted with long rests, as in Exercises 125 and 127.

Dotted Eighth & 16th Note

Exercises **131–140**

To play Ex. 132 the way a classical player would, think in 16th notes: the dotted eighth gets three, the last 16th note, one.

Straight

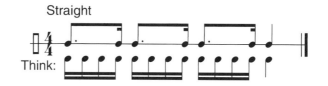

Think:

Grieg's famous "Humoresque" is a good example of the dotted eighth plus 16th figure in classical music. For the swing feel, the rhythm is "softened." The dotted eighth is played a hair shorter and the 16th a hair longer than is mathematically correct. Exercise 132 contains the shuffle beat as used in "Bad, Bad Leroy Brown," "Kansas City" and others.

It may be helpful to think of the syllables "humpty dumpty, humpty dumpty" or "Da-ma, da-ma" when playing this rhythm.

(continued on next page)

"Humoresque" by Edvard Grieg

Track 14.1, Straight Feel
Track 14.2, Swing Feel

Dotted Eighth & 16th Note (cont.)

Exercises **141–150**

The dotted-eighth-16th figure is also the basis for the ride cymbal beat perfected by Jo Jones of the Count Basie band in the 1930s. It was one of the things that gave that band its tremendous swing.

Ride cymbal

Bass drum

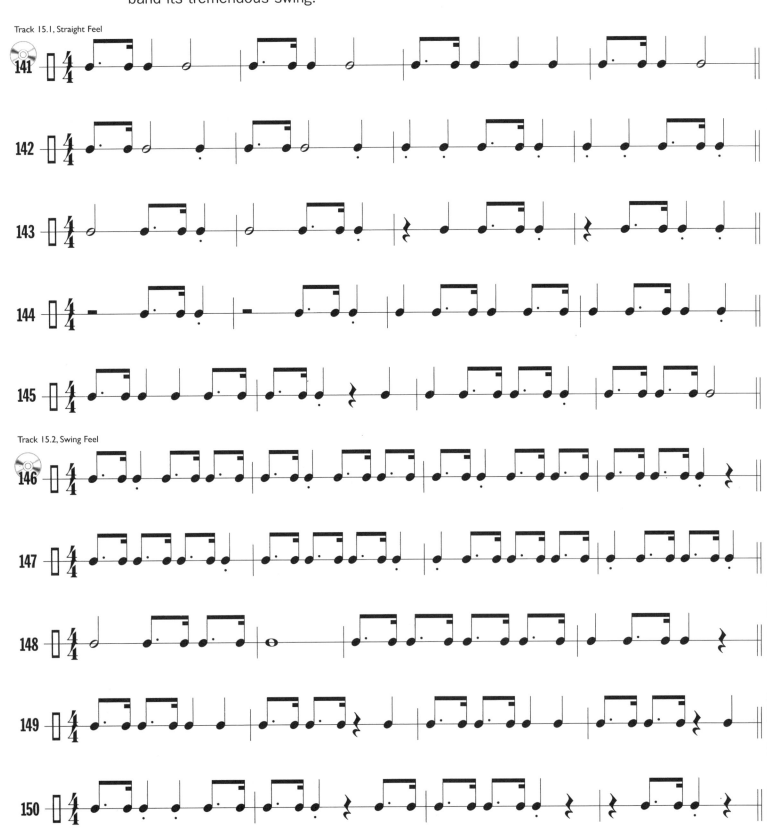

16th Notes & 16th Rests

Exercises
151–160

The 16th rest is almost always used in a variant of the rhythms on pages 23–26. A 16th note followed by a 16th rest is played like an eighth note with a staccato dot, that is, a very short eighth note. For example, measure 2 of Ex. 151 could be sung "tuck-a tuck, tuck-a-tuck." Measure 4 could be sung "tuck tuck-a, tuck tuck-a, tuck tuck-a, tuck."

Played the same as

Track 16, Straight Feel

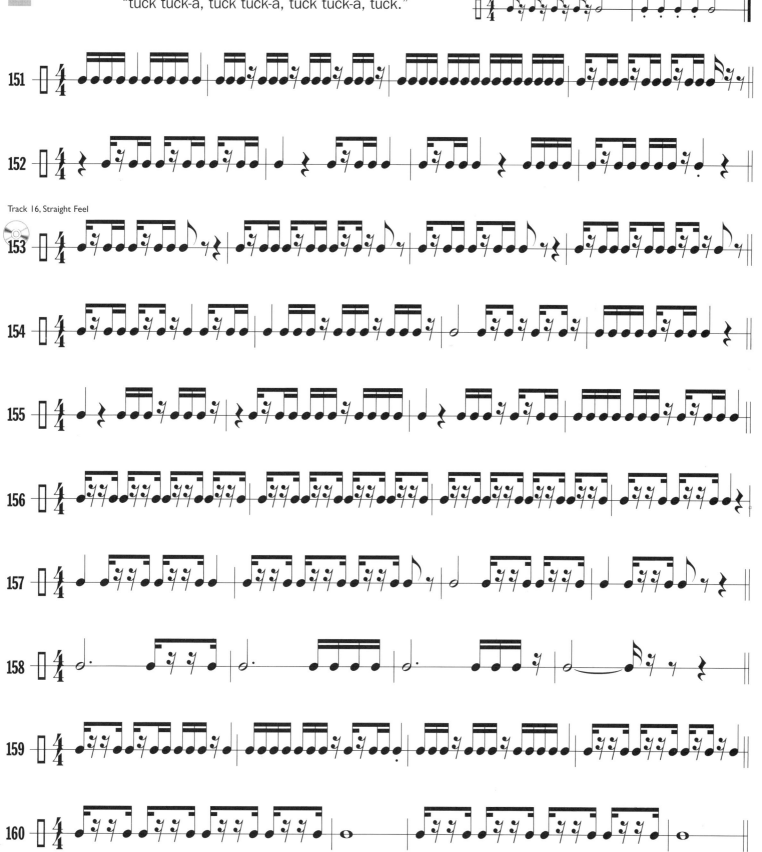

Dotted Eighths & 16ths & Eighth Note Triplets

Exercises **161–170**

Strictly speaking, the 16th note of a dotted-eighth-16th-note figure is played a fraction of a second later than the last note of an eighth note triplet. See, for example, Beethoven's famous "Moonlight Sonata."

In the swing feel, however, the dotted-eighth-16th-note figure is played much the same as the triplet.

Track 17.1, Straight Feel
Track 17.2, Swing Feel

Eighths, 16ths & Eighth Note Triplets

Exercises 171–180

This page of exercises illustrates the subtle—but important—differences among these three rhythms. Although each figure presents three notes in one beat, they are all different. Since there is no appreciable difference in interpretation between the swing and straight feel of these figures, you need only practice this page with a straight feel.

Track 18, Straight Feel

Double-Dotted Quarter & 16th Notes

Exercises 181–190

The single dot extends the time value of a note by half. The second dot adds a half of a half. The double-dotted quarter note is the same as a quarter note plus an eighth note plus a 16th note.

This rhythm can be written either way. Thus Exercises 181 and 182 are played identically. It is always helpful to tap or click for the first dot.

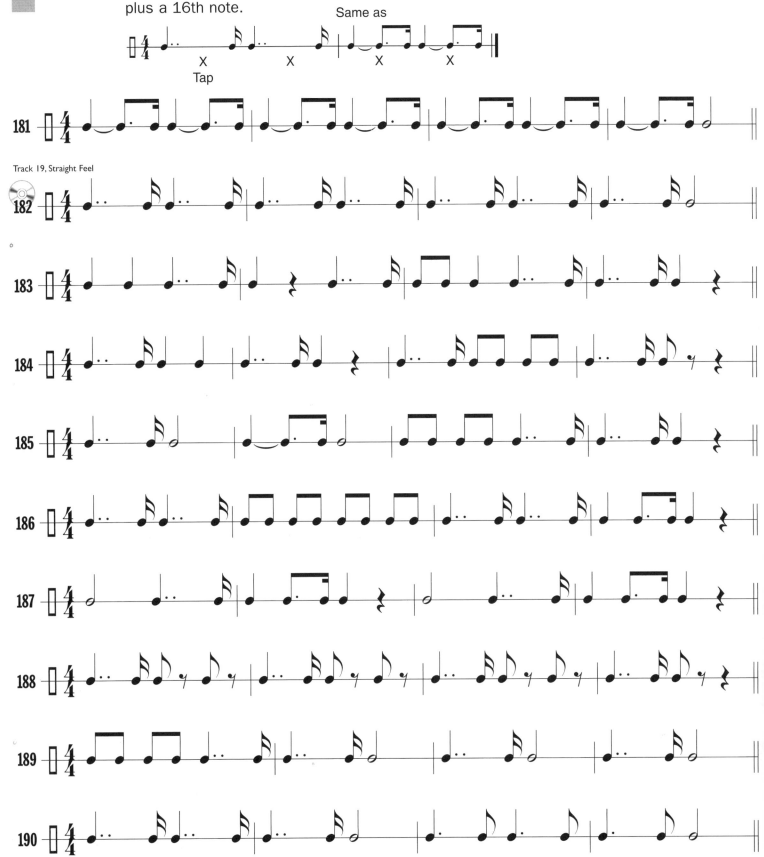

Quarter Note Triplets

Exercises
191–200

The quarter-note triplet is a group of three quarter notes played in the time of two, that is, in two beats (in 4/4 time).

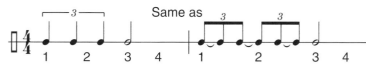

Start with two eighth-note triplets and accent every other note as in Ex. 191.

Then, tie the eighth notes together as follows: first & second, third & fourth, and fifth & sixth as in Ex. 192. If done correctly, this will sound exactly like Ex. 193. Keep the quarter triplets even; do not allow them to become a quarter and two eighths or two eighths and a quarter.

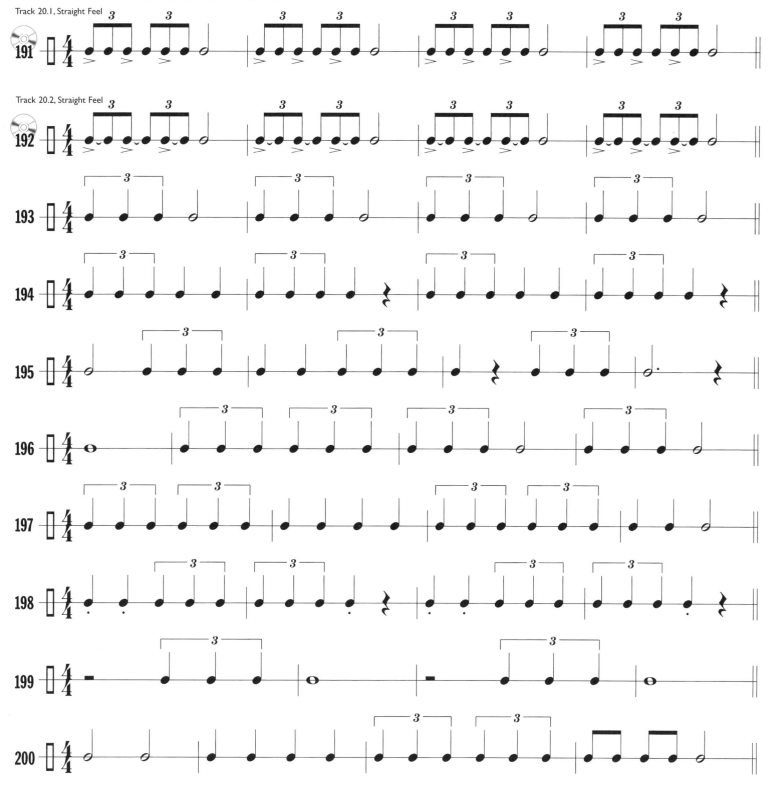

Quarter Note Triplets & Eighth Notes

Exercises
201–210

These exercises contrast quarter-note triplets with various figures of eighth notes, dotted quarters and 16ths. Keep the quarter-note triplets smooth and even and resist the tendency to rush the eighth notes.

Track 21.1, Straight Feel
Track 21.2, Swing Feel

Quarter Note Triplets, Eighth Note Triplets & 16th Notes

Exercises
211–220

Contrasting quarter note triplets with eighth-note triplets is relatively easy, because both rhythms divide the measure in multiples of three. Much more difficult is contrasting triplets and figures such as eighth or 16th notes, which divide the measure into multiples of two and four. Practice this page carefully with your metronome. Make sure you can play the whole page without stopping before moving on to page 34.

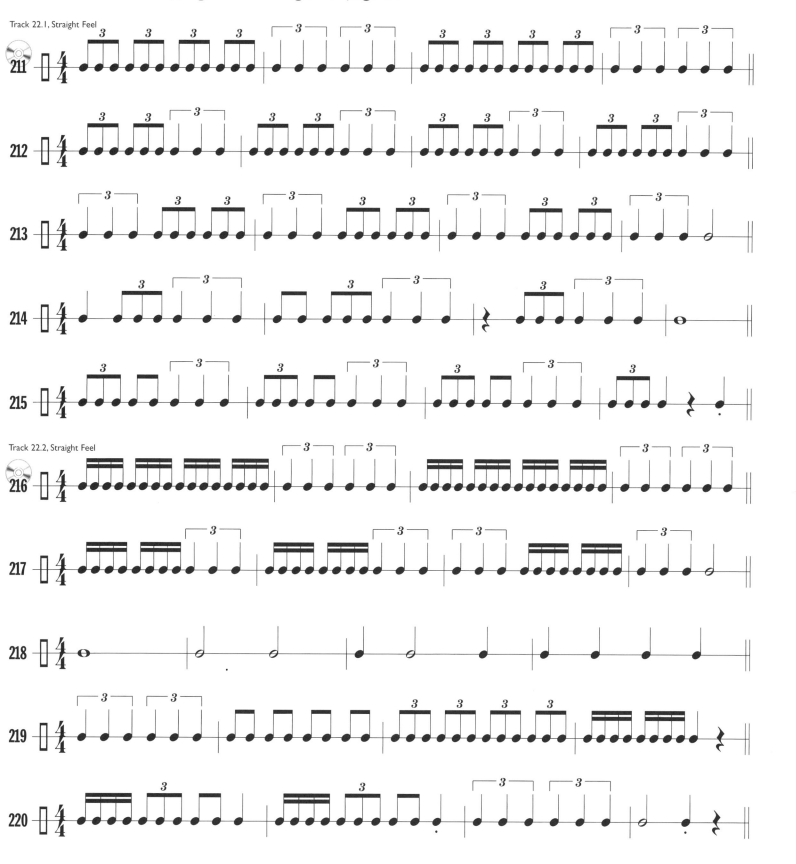

Eighth Notes Coming In Off the Beat

Exercises **221–230**

Here is where you'll find that foot taps (or tongue clicks) will come in handy. If the eighth note comes on the "&" of beat one (Exercises 221–225), tap on beat one.

If the eighth note comes in on the "&" of beat 2 (Exercises 226 and 227), tap on beats 1 and 2.

If the eighth note comes in on the "&" of beat 3 (Ex. 230), tap on beats 1, 2 and 3. (continued on p. 35)

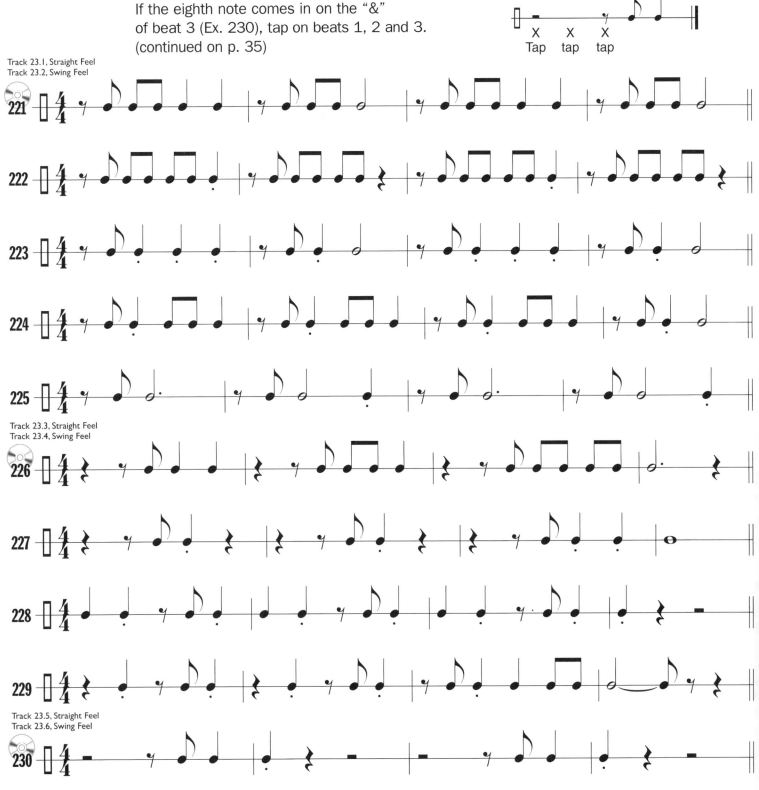

Track 23.1, Straight Feel
Track 23.2, Swing Feel

Track 23.3, Straight Feel
Track 23.4, Swing Feel

Track 23.5, Straight Feel
Track 23.6, Swing Feel

Off-the-Beat Eighth Notes, Ties & Triplets

Exercises
231–240

If the eighth note comes in on the "&" of beat 4 (Ex. 231) tap on beats 1, 2, 3 and 4. This is an important technique for playing pickups correctly:

When rests occur on beats in the middle of a measure (Exercises 228, 229, 232 and others), it's always helpful to tap for the rest.

Track 24.1, Straight Feel
Track 24.2, Swing Feel

Track 24.3, Straight Feel
Track 24.4 Swing Feel

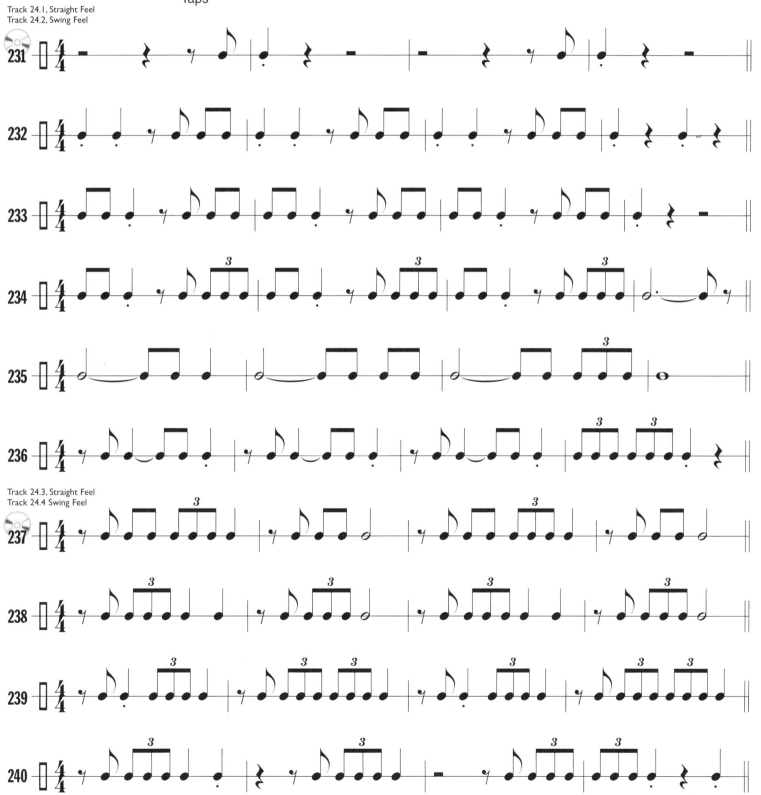

Various Notes Tied Across the Barline to Eighth Notes

Exercises 241–250

In every case where a note is tied across a bar line—especially to an eighth note—it's important to tap for the tied note, as in Exercises 241 and 242.

Track 25.1, Straight Feel
Track 25.2, Swing Feel

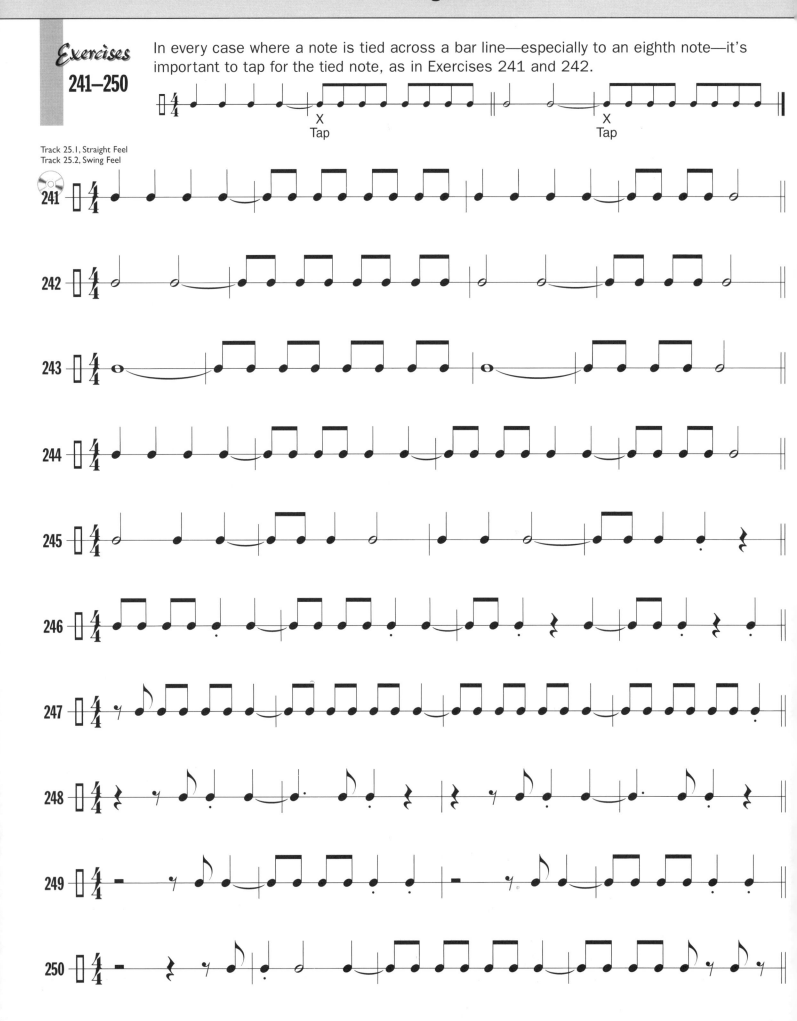

Variations On Eighth-Note Triplets

Exercises **251–260**

Triplets can be varied in several ways: Notes may be tied; if two eighth notes are tied in the same beat they are written as a quarter note (Exercises 251, 252, 256).

One or more of the notes in the triplet may be replaced by a rest (Exercises 253, 254, 255).

A longer note may be tied to the first note of the triplet (Exercises 258–260). Especially in this case, a tap will help you get the figure right.

Variations On Quarter-Note Triplets

Exercises
261–270

Everything said about eighth-note triplets can be applied to quarter-note triplets as well. Always use foot taps in places where there is a tie (Exercises 261–263) or where the measure begins with a rest (Ex. 264). Of special note is a figure that occurs in Ex. 268. This is a sub-divided triplet which should be played.

Ex. 268, measure 1

Think:

Track 27, Straight Feel

Half-Note Triplets

Exercises
271–280 Half-note triplets are not seen very often but they have been used in quite a few show tunes, notably "I Get a Kick Out of You" and "Everything's Coming Up Roses." One way to count half-note triplets accurately is to start with quarter note triplets (Ex. 271, measure 1). Then tie the notes together in groups of two (Ex. 271, measure 2). Measure 2 and measure 3 are played identically. Exercises 278–280 are a quick summary of just about everything discussed in this book so far.

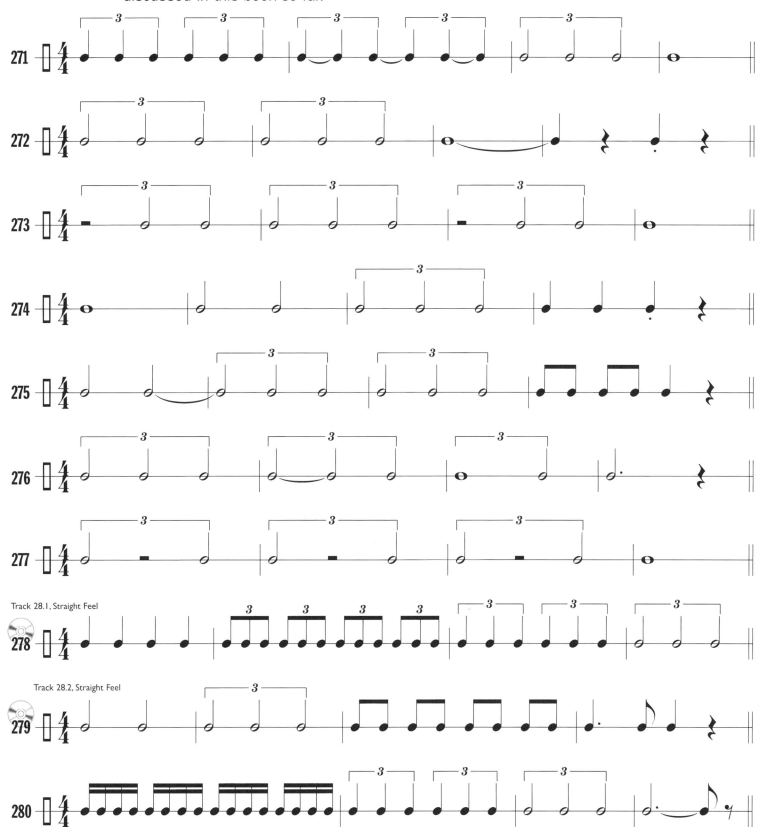

PART TWO : Single Syncopation

A Brief History of Syncopation in American Jazz and Popular Music

The word *syncopation* is defined (in Grove's Dictionary of Music) as "An alteration of the normal time accents of the bar by the setting up of contrary accents." Although this definition is adequate for classical music[1], it is incomplete with regard to jazz, swing and American popular music. The so-called "swing feel," which we have already met when playing eighth notes, makes a subtle but crucial difference in the way syncopations are played. Each syncopated note is actually an anticipation of a note normally heard on the downbeat. That is, a note that might be expected on the third beat of the measure is actually played earlier, just after the upbeat of the second beat; because it is in an unexpected place, the note is accented slightly (see page 41).

The first American musicians to make extensive use of syncopation seem to have been African-American pianists living in the Southwest. A few years after the Civil War, and certainly by 1885, pianists in St. Louis and other towns were using an effect in which certain notes of the melody were played a little before the downbeat on which they were expected. This effect was called "ragging the time" or "ragged time," which was soon shortened to "ragtime." With the publication of the first ragtime pieces in the 1890s such as "At a Georgia Camp-meeting" by Kerry Mills and especially the huge hit "Maple Leaf Rag"[2] by Scott Joplin, ragtime became a national, and later an international, craze. Even classical composers such as Claude Debussy (1862–1918) and Igor Stravinsky (1882–1971) incorporated ragtime into their works "Golliwog's Cakewalk" (1908) and "L'Histoire du Soldat" (1917) respectively. Other composers such as Darius Milhaud ("Le Boeuf sur le Toit") and Kurt Weill ("The Threepenny Opera") continued this tradition well into the modern era.

To modern ears, ragtime sounds rhythmically rather stiff. This may be, however, because it is generally interpreted by classically trained pianists who play the syncopations as written—exactly off the beat, rather than the more relaxed way a jazz musician might play them. This writer was told by the daughter of composer W. C. Handy ("St. Louis Blues" [1914]) that pianists around the turn of the century had a freer interpretation of the beat than was written down, and actually played eighth notes very much like jazz players do today, long-short, long-short. In any case, ragtime, which had started out as piano music, was soon arranged for marching bands and dance orchestras. In this way, and with the great popularity of such ragtime-influenced songs as "Bill Bailey" (1902) and "Alexander's Ragtime Band" (1911), syncopated rhythms gradually entered the consciousness of the American listening public.

Around the time of World War I (1914–1918) the ragtime craze began to fade and was replaced by blues and jazz in the public's affection. These art forms relied heavily on ragtime rhythms, as is obvious in songs like "Basin Street Blues" and "A Good Man Is Hard to Find," both from 1917. A group of five white musicians from New Orleans who called themselves "The Original Dixieland Jazz Band" was the first "jass"[3] band to be recorded on the primitive equipment of the day. The success of their recordings "Tiger Rag" and "Livery Stable Blues," and their sensational debut at Reisenweber's Restaurant in New York in 1919, did much to popularize instrumental ragtime and early jazz and blues. However, their interpretation of eighth notes, while not quite as stiff as ragtime, did not have the relaxed flow of later artists.

Jelly Roll Morton, whose real name was Ferdinand LaMenthe (1885–1941), was a New Orleans born pianist who liked to brag that he had invented jazz. Coming from anyone else this might have sounded ludicrous, but Mr. Jelly was one of the great pianists of the 20th century. Even his earliest recordings in 1923 show a smooth, relaxed flow of eighth notes quite different from the stilted rhythms of ragtime, so his boast may have had a basis in fact. But the most important figure in the development of the swing feel was the beloved cornetist, trumpeter, singer and entertainer, Louis "Satchmo" Armstrong. After making some important recordings as a sideman with his mentor, jazz legend Joe "King" Oliver in the early 1920s, and after a short stint with Fletcher Henderson's groundbreaking orchestra, Armstrong made a series of recordings with his own small groups, the "Hot Five" and the "Hot Seven" that are breathtaking even today. His solos soar above the somewhat plodding rhythm section with a freshness and rhythmic swing that revolutionized the whole concept of how to play jazz. He was the most influential figure in the history of this music, and every subsequent player owes Satchmo an enormous debt. His ideas were soon emulated not only by trumpet players like Red Allen and Louis Prima, but by other jazz greats such as pianist Earl Hines, trombonist Jack Teagarden, clarinetists Jimmie Noone and Benny Goodman, saxophonists Benny Carter and Coleman Hawkins, and singers Billie Holiday, Peggy Lee, Bing Crosby and the Boswell Sisters. In later years, even beboppers like Charlie Parker and Dizzy Gillespie acknowledged their debt to the great Satchmo.

The 1930s and 1940s saw the rhythms of early jazz incorporated into the big bands of the day. Many of the most popular bands were led by musicians who were either jazz players themselves or who had the sense to hire the best talent around. These include Duke Ellington, Count Basie, Jimmie Lunceford, Benny Goodman, Artie Shaw, Tommy and Jimmy Dorsey, Glenn Miller and many others. It was at this time that the demands made on band musicians were increased to include the ability to read complicated syncopations at sight. Even more demanding were the bebop charts that began to be played around 1946, as these were not only rhythmically complex, but were often performed at breakneck tempos.

Since the decline of the big dance bands after World War II, so-called stage bands have become very popular. There are thousands of young players in these bands at high schools and colleges that play the challenging modern arrangements of Sammy Nestico, Dave Wolpe, Dave Barduhn and so many others. These arrangements require players to read syncopated figures at sight, often at blinding speed.

The sections that follow analyze hundreds of examples of syncopations and other challenging rhythmic figures.

[1]Classical musicians are trained to play this displaced note directly on the up-beat rather than a little after it as jazz players do. This tends to give the classical guys a rather stilted sound when they try to play jazz. Listen to most recordings of Gershwin's "Rhapsody in Blue" or "An American in Paris" to hear what we mean.

[2]Contrary to popular opinion, the "Maple Leaf Rag" has nothing to do with Canada. It was named after a gin mill in St. Louis.

[3]With its sexual implications, the word "jazz" was considered too risqué in 1917 to be used on a record label. On the ODJB's early recordings the word is spelled "jass."

Playing Syncopations

As previously mentioned, syncopations played in jazz with the swing feel are actually anticipations of a note. For example, think of two half notes: the first is played on the downbeat of "1" and the second on the downbeat of "3."

This figure, of course, does not have any syncopation. If we anticipate the second note we get the following figure:

This has important implications.

1. When counting, this means that since the anticipated note is really the third beat of the measure, *the next number is 4, not 3.* This is important because it is very easy to mis-count when playing syncopations.

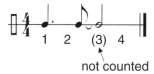

2. Since the anticipated note is a displaced downbeat, all syncopations should be accented. Sometimes arrangers indicate this, other times they take it for granted. In this book we give many examples of each, but remember to accent all syncopations, marked or not.

We have classified all the syncopations in this book according to the anticipated notes. The first exercises in this section, numbers 281–470, deal with the anticipated third beat of the measure. This particular syncopation was brought to the Western Hemisphere by black slaves from West Africa, where it is an integral part of the folk music. The anticipated third beat is characteristic of a dizzying array of music, including *Latin-American* rhumba, cha-cha, son montuno, bolero, merengue and calypso; *Brazilian* samba, baion and bossa nova and *Argentine* tango. In America, the same anticipated third beat has been a part of ragtime, the Charleston and early rock and roll. Its importance cannot be overstated.

Anticipated 3rd Beat

Exercises 281–290

Exercise 281 contrasts a non-syncopated measure (measure 1) with a syncopated version of the same rhythm (measure 2). Make sure you can play this exercise before going on to the more complex examples, and remember to accent the syncopations even though they aren't marked.

Track 29.1, Straight Feel
Track 29.2, Swing Feel

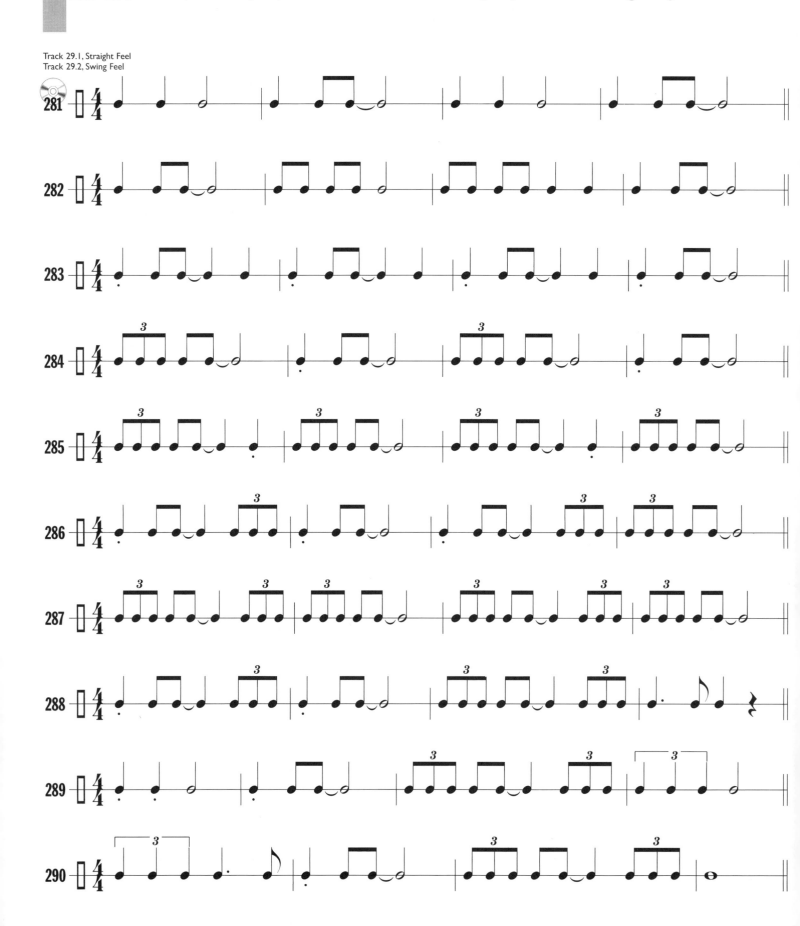

Anticipated 3rd Beat (cont.)

Exercises
291–300

Exercise 292 demonstrates the calypso beat. Guitarists can use this rhythm as their calypso strum pattern.

You'll also notice it's used in calypso melodies such as the verse of "Jamaica Farewell."

Track 30.1, Straight Feel
Track 30.2, Swing Feel

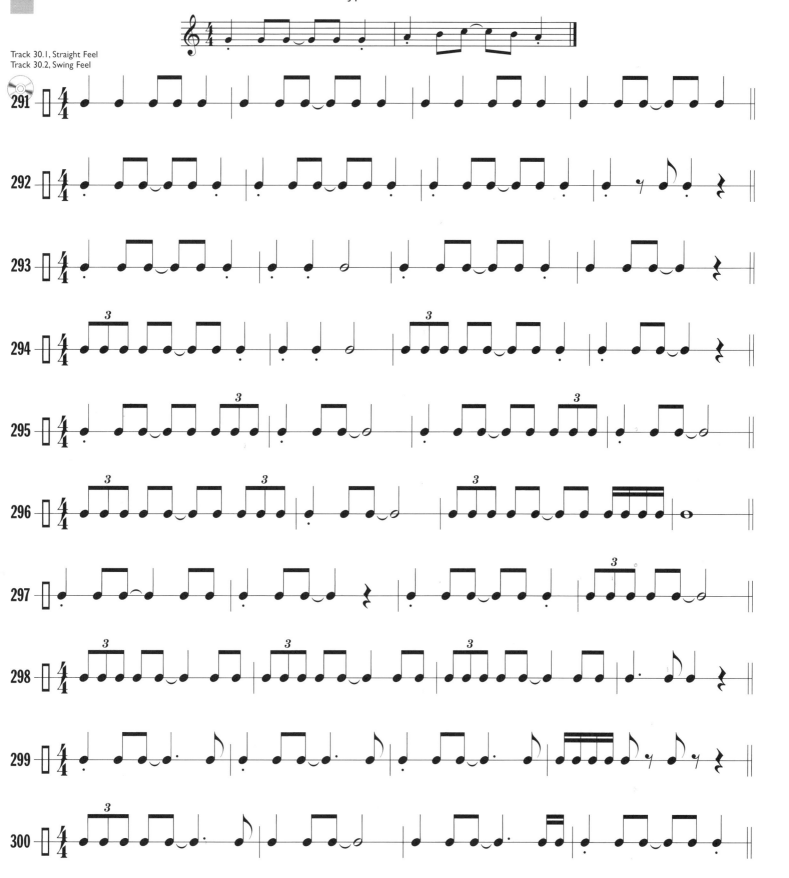

Anticipated 3rd Beat (cont.)

Exercises **301–310**

Exercise 301 contains a variation on the basic calypso beat. Guitarists can use it as a strum pattern.

It also appears in many calypso-style melodies such as the chorus of "Jamaica Farewell."

Track 31.1, Straight Feel
Track 31.2, Swing Feel

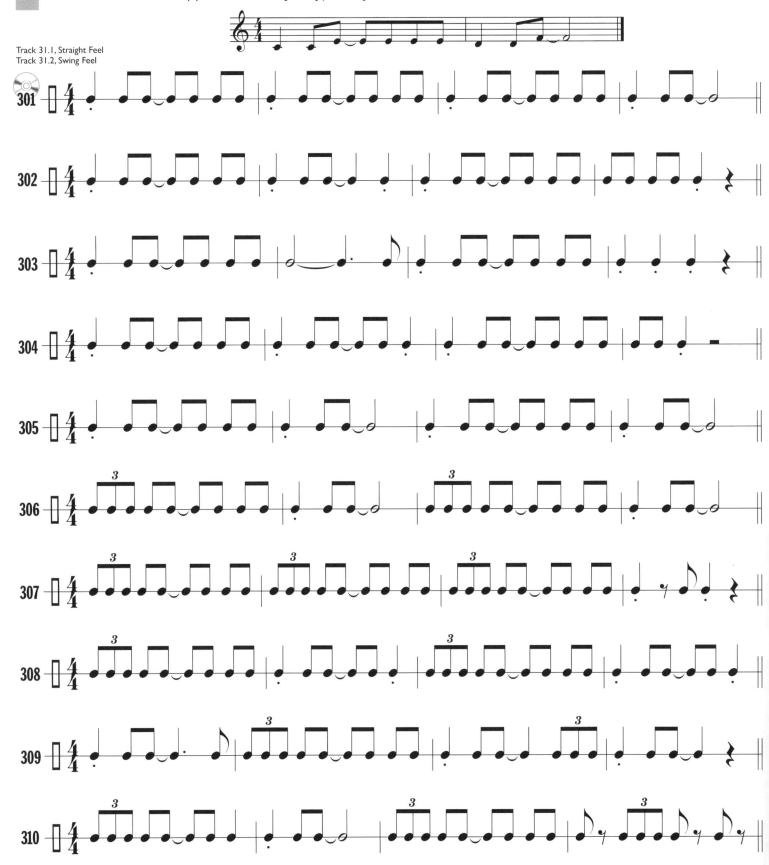

Anticipated 3rd Beat (cont.)

Exercises
311–320

If helpful, you may think of Ex. 311 as a syncopated version of this simple figure.

Don't forget to accent the syncopated note.

Track 32.1, Straight Feel
Track 32.2, Swing Feel

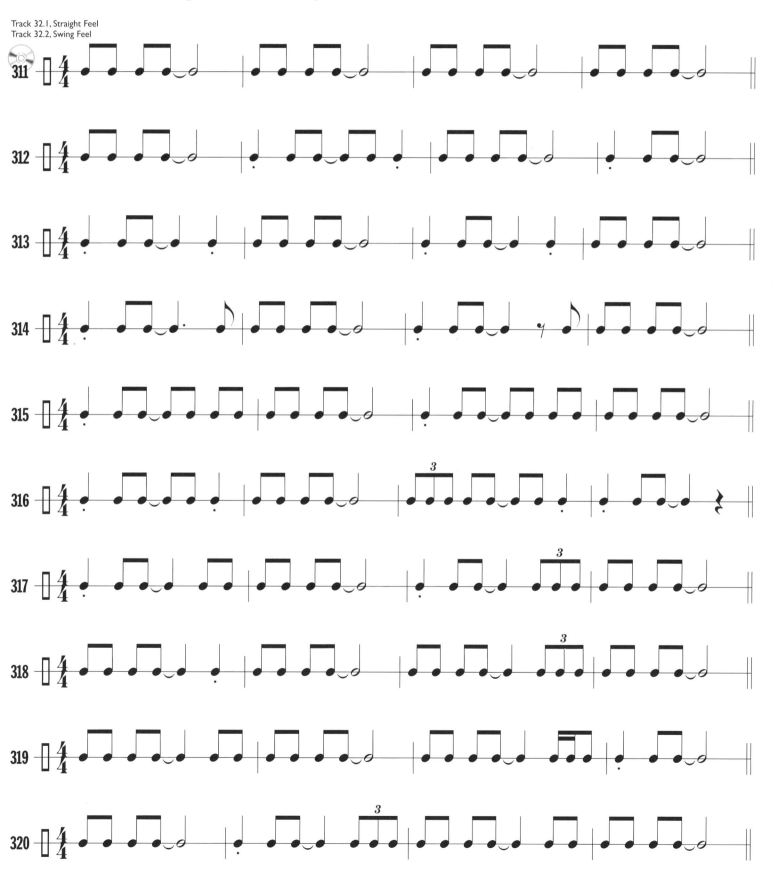

Anticipated 3rd Beat (cont.)

Exercises
321–330

These syncopations review and expand the previous pages. You may want to create melodic versions of these rhythms. For example, Ex. 325 could become.

Exercise 329 might become.

Track 33.1, Straight Feel
Track 33.2, Swing Feel

Anticipated 3rd Beat (cont.)

Exercises 331–340

Exercise 331 is the anticipated third beat in its purest form. The "Charleston" became a dance craze in the 1920s and is still played occasionally. The opening measures of the chorus use Ex. 331 note for note.

Exercise 332 is the same figure with the first note shortened a bit. The rest of the page deals with variations of this same figure.

Track 34.1, Straight Feel
Track 34.2, Swing Feel

Anticipated 3rd Beat Combined with Rests on the Downbeat

Exercises
341–350

When starting with a rest, tap or click for the missing beat(s). One tap for Exercises 341–343 and 347–350.

and two taps for Exercises 344–346.

Anticipated 3rd Beat Tied to Various Triplet Figures

Exercises **351–360**

These figures won't give you any trouble if you foot tap for the tied note as in the first measures of Exercises 351 and 352. You can create melodic fragments with any of these figures. For example, Ex. 358 might become:

Track 36, Swing Feel

Anticipated 3rd Beat & Ties Over the Barline

Exercises
361–370

Here again foot taps or tongue clicks on tied notes are the key to playing these exercises accurately. Don't forget to create melodic fragments with some or all of the exercises. Exercise 365 might become:

Exercises 366 through 370 are designed to be played as one unit.
That is, the last measure of each flows directly into the next exercise.

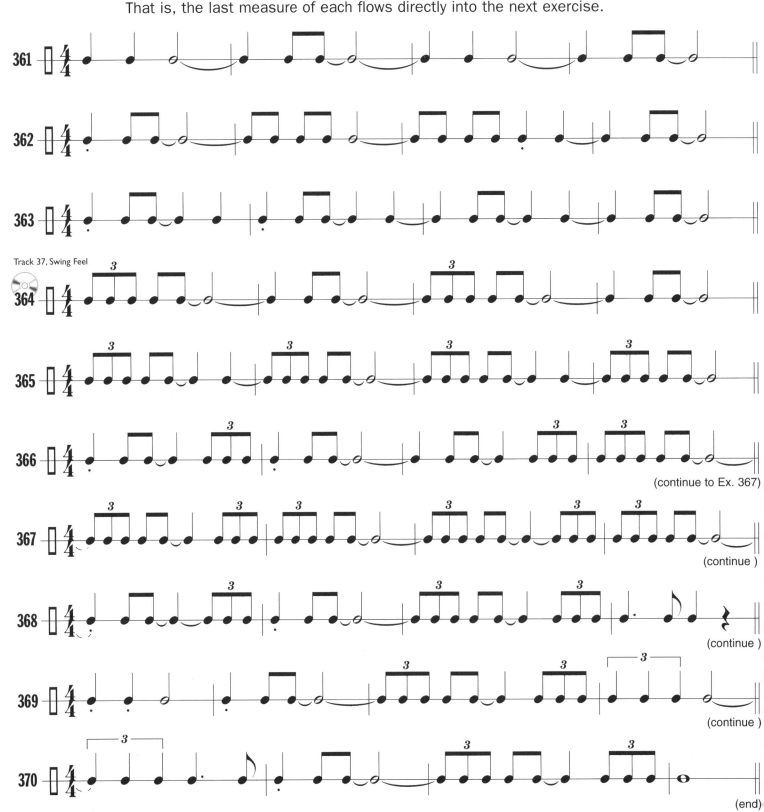

Track 37, Swing Feel

(continue to Ex. 367)

(continue)

(continue)

(continue)

(end)

Anticipated 3rd Beat & Ties Over the Barline (cont.)

Exercises
371–380

Let Ex. 371 flow directly into Ex. 372. Exercises 376 through 378 can and should be practiced as one unit. Here's a melodic version of Exercises 376 and 377. Now create your own.

Track 38, Swing Feel

Anticipated 3rd Beat in Staccato Notation

Exercises **381–390**

Many modern arrangers use what's sometimes called "staccato notation." In this type of notation, a figure that has traditionally been written as:

is notated as:

Since the tied note on the first figure is generally cut off short, both figures are played pretty much the same. This allows arrangers to save time by omitting the tie and additional note. For the player, however, this may cause some confusion. For example, measure 1 of Ex. 381 looks as though the second eighth note is left hanging. But that note is actually the anticipation of the 3rd beat and therefore must be accented. Many more examples of staccato notation follow.

Track 39, Swing Feel

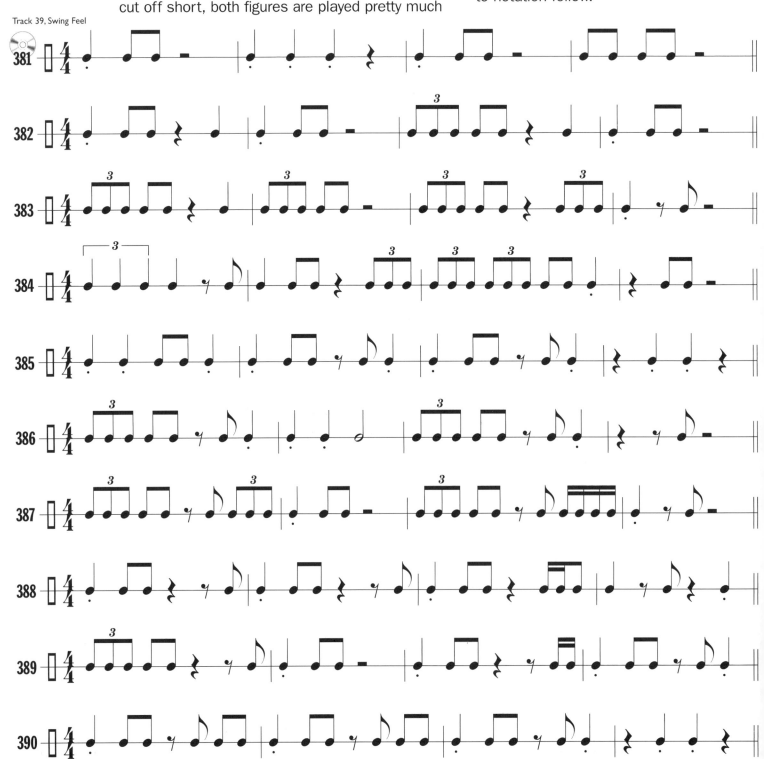

Anticipated 3rd Beat in Staccato Notation (cont.)

Exercises
391–400

Generally speaking, every time you see an off-beat eighth note followed by a rest, you can assume that it is the anticipation of a note and must be accented. There are examples of this in virtually every measure on this page.

Track 40.1, Straight Feel
Track 40.2, Swing Feel

Anticipated 3rd Beat in Staccato Notation (cont.)

Exercises 401–410

Here are more examples of staccato notation. Exercise 401 is a staccato version of the Charleston rhythm on page 47. Exercises 407 and 409 test the truth of the old adage that rests are harder to play than notes. Be especially careful when starting with a rest, as in Exercises 407–410.

Track 41.1, Straight Feel
Track 41.2, Swing Feel

Anticipated 3rd Beat in Staccato Notation with Extensive Rests

Exercises 411–420

This whole page is especially valuable for brass players, who are often called upon to punctuate the melody with figures such as these. Here's a melodic example with the saxes playing long held notes as the trumpets and trombones play a figure based on Ex. 417.

Track 42.1, Straight Feel
Track 42.2, Swing Feel

Anticipated 3rd Beat in Staccato Notation with Broken Triplets

Exercises
421–430

Initial rests add to the complexity of the examples on this page. Always mark them with a foot tap or tongue click. Ex. 430 is a typical pickup figure, which often appears something like:

Tap twice for missing
two beats of pickup measure

Track 43.1, Straight Feel
Track 43.2, Swing Feel

Anticipated 3rd Beat as Part of an Eighth Note Triplet

Exercises 431–440

Since the swing feel demands that off-beat eighth notes be played a little late, the difference between:

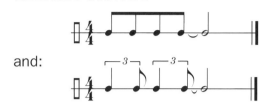

and:

is negligible; however, when practicing this with the straight eighth feel, the difference is very noticeable. Watch out for tricky examples like Exercises 435–438 and 440 that start with a rest. By now, you should know how to deal with them.

Track 44.1, Straight Feel
Track 44.2, Swing Feel

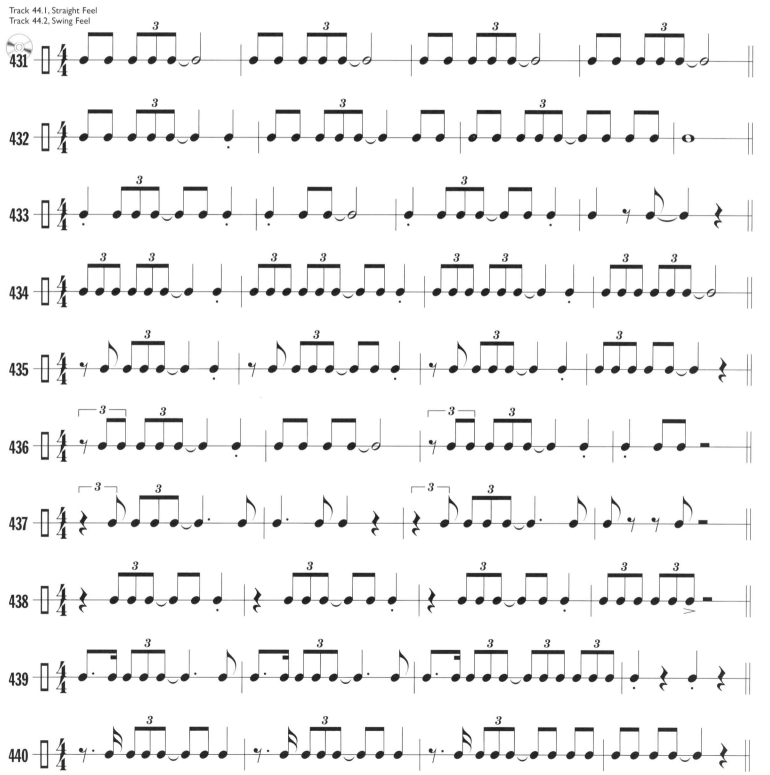

Anticipated 3rd Beat as Part of a Quarter Note Triplet

Exercises
441–450

Here is a very challenging group of exercises. Remember to tap or click for all tied notes and rests. Create your own melodic examples. Exercise 449 might sound like this:

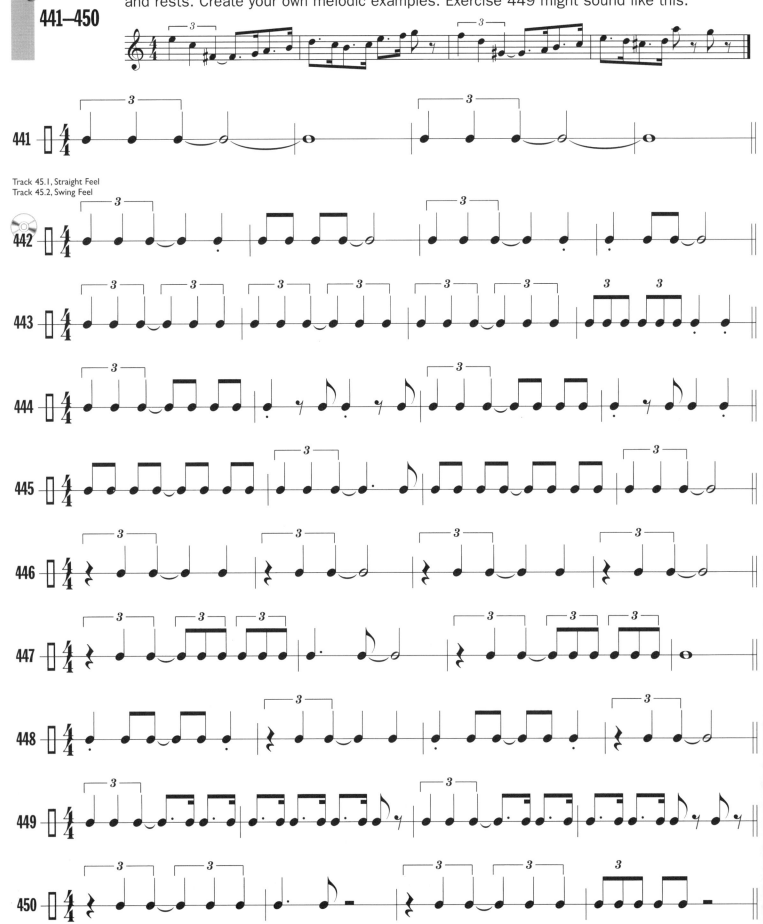

Track 45.1, Straight Feel
Track 45.2, Swing Feel

Anticipated 3rd Beat *&* Dotted Eighths *&* 16ths

Exercises
451–460

Jazz players usually "soften" the dotted-eighth-16th-note figure to something like:

Keep this in mind when practicing this entire page. Practically speaking, the swing feel tends to make the following three figures sound almost identical.

Track 46, Swing Feel

Anticipated 3rd Beat, Downbeat Rests *&* Dotted Eighths *&* 16ths

Exercises
461–470

Tap or click for every missing beat, especially when the number of silent beats is high as in Exercises 466 and 470. Many of the figures on this page are typical of brass punctuations like this version of Ex. 466: the saxes play the melody while the brass punctuates.

Track 47.1, Straight Feel
Track 47.2, Swing Feel

Anticipated 2nd Beat

Exercises 471–480

The following pages deal with the anticipated 2nd beat. The eighth-quarter-eighth figure is very common to all types of music. The folk song "Tom Dooley" starts with it, as does "Rudolph, the Red-Nosed Reindeer."

Even though the second note is written as a quarter, it is usually shortened to an eighth note followed by an eighth rest.

played as

To get the proper feel for this rhythm, think of the first two measures of "Rudolph" and then sing the first two measures of Ex. 472.

Track 48.1, Straight Feel
Track 48.2, Swing Feel

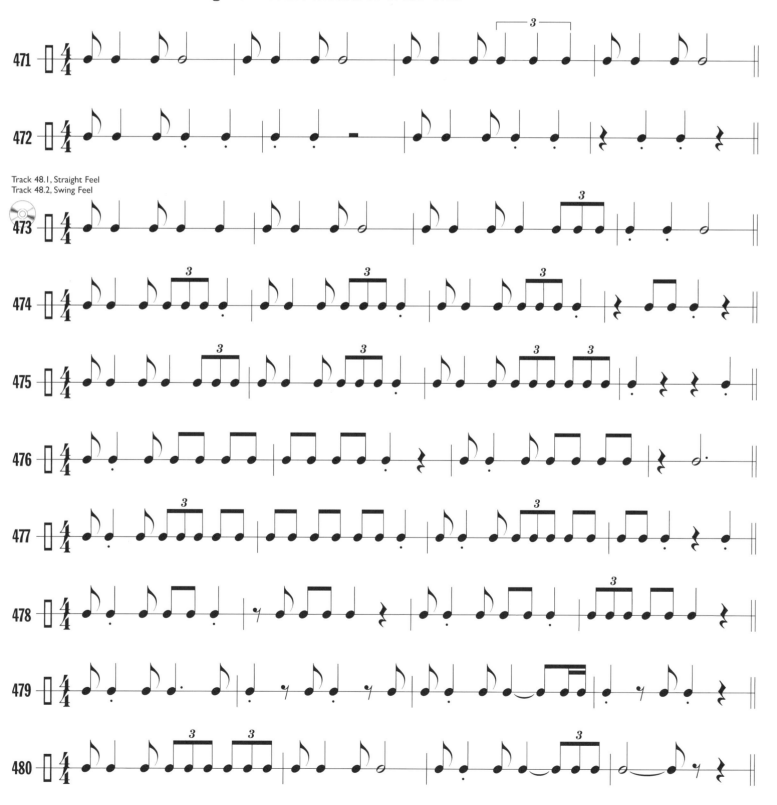

Anticipated 2nd Beat (cont.)

Exercises 481–490

The downbeat eighth note followed by a longer note is characteristic of some types of folk music, especially Scottish ("Comin' Thro' the Rye") and Hungarian ("Czardas"). Don't shorten the second note unless it is marked with a staccato dot, as in Ex. 482. Exercise 484 introduces the tenuto mark (–). When this dash is placed above or below a note it means to hold the note for its full value and give it a slight accent.

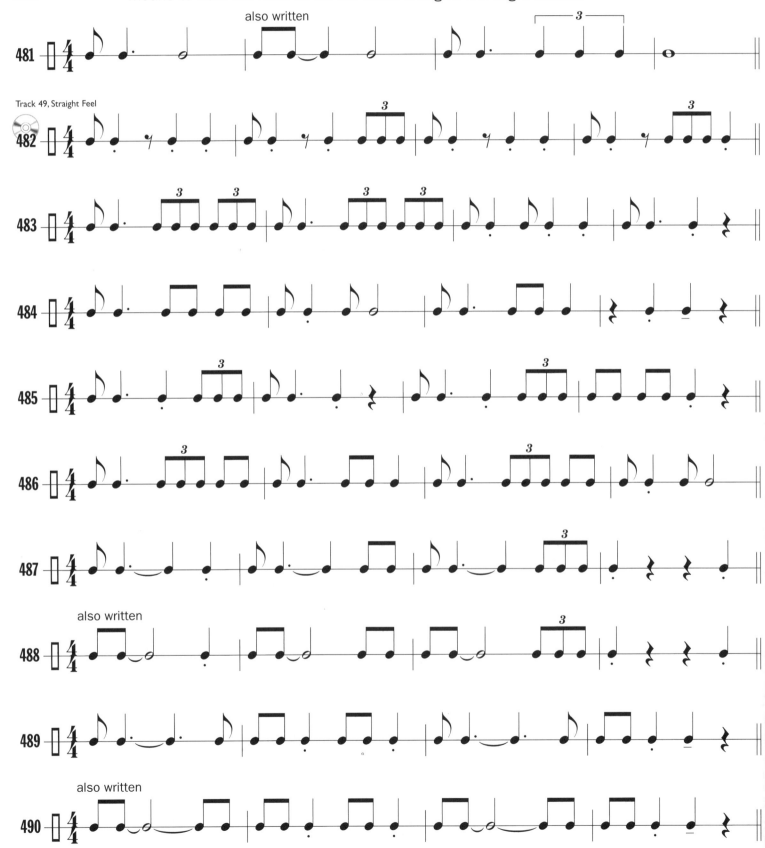

Anticipated 2nd Beat Starting Off the Beat

Exercises 491–500

An eighth rest replaces the initial eighth note in this version of the anticipated 2nd beat. Always tap or click on the rest, and the figure won't give you any trouble:

Exercise 494 introduces the *marcato* or "hat" accent (∧). It is a shorter and sharper version of the accent (>).

Track 50, Swing Feel

Anticipated 2nd Beat Starting Off the Beat (cont.)

Exercises
501–510

Exercises 501–508 contain typical brass punctuations.
Here's how Ex. 501 might be used to punctuate a sax melody.

Track 51, Swing Feel

Anticipated 2nd Beat, Ties & Staccato Notation

Exercises
511–520

Here's how the anticipated 2nd beat looks in staccato notation.

Remember to accent any off-beat eighth notes that are followed by rests. Exercise 512 introduces the "hat" accent in combination with the staccato dot. It means to accent a note and cut it off as short as possible.

Track 52.1, Straight Feel
Track 52.2, Swing Feel

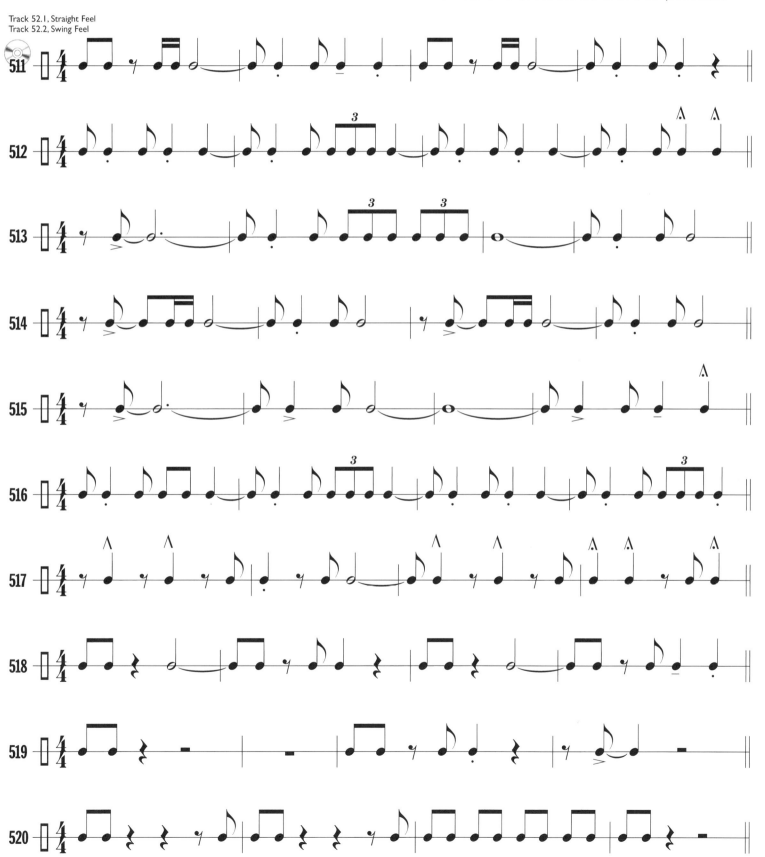

Anticipated 2nd or 3rd Beat

Exercises
521–530

This page mixes the anticipated 3rd beat with the anticipated 2nd beat (but not in the same measure). Try creating your own melodies. For example, Ex. 525 might sound like this.

Track 53, Swing Feel

Anticipated 3rd or 2nd Beat & Initial Rests

Exercises
531–540

As usual, when figures begin with rests, mark the downbeat with a foot tap or tongue click. Ex. 536 might be used for punctuating brass figures.

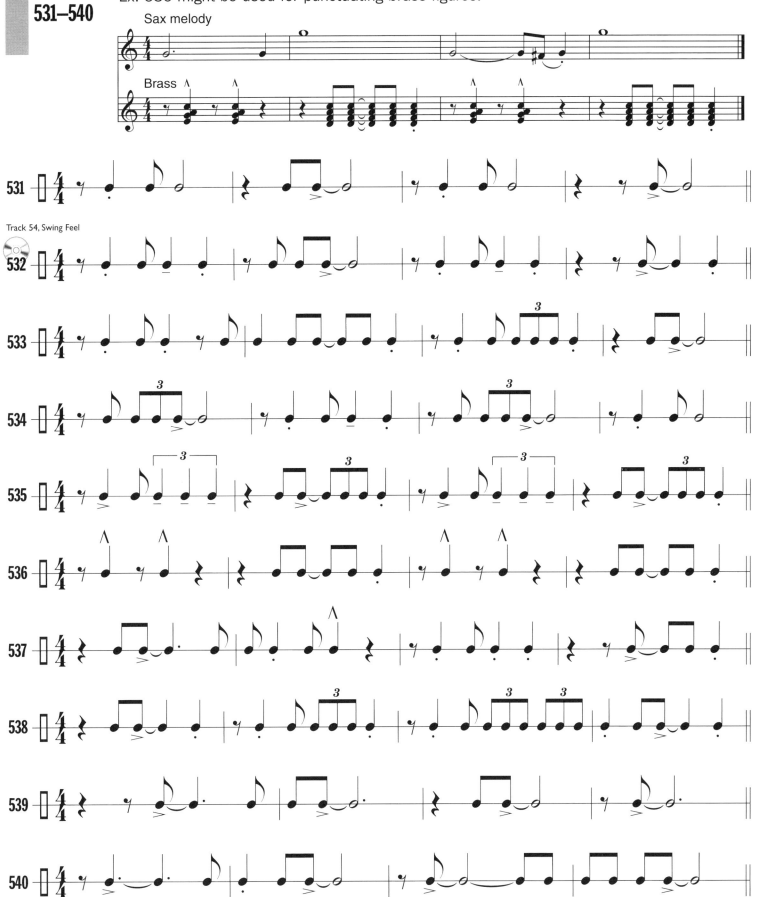

Anticipated 2nd or 3rd Beat & Ties Over the Barline

Exercises
541–550

As usual, when notes are tied over the barline, tap or click for the tied notes. See the following example of how to do this for Ex. 541.

Track 55, Swing Feel

Anticipated 2nd or 3rd Beat in Staccato Notation

Exercises 551–560

Every figure on this page may be seen as a brass punctuation or comping (an improvised chordal accompaniment) pattern for guitar or keyboard. For example, here's how Ex. 551 might be used to comp the first four bars of a blues in F.

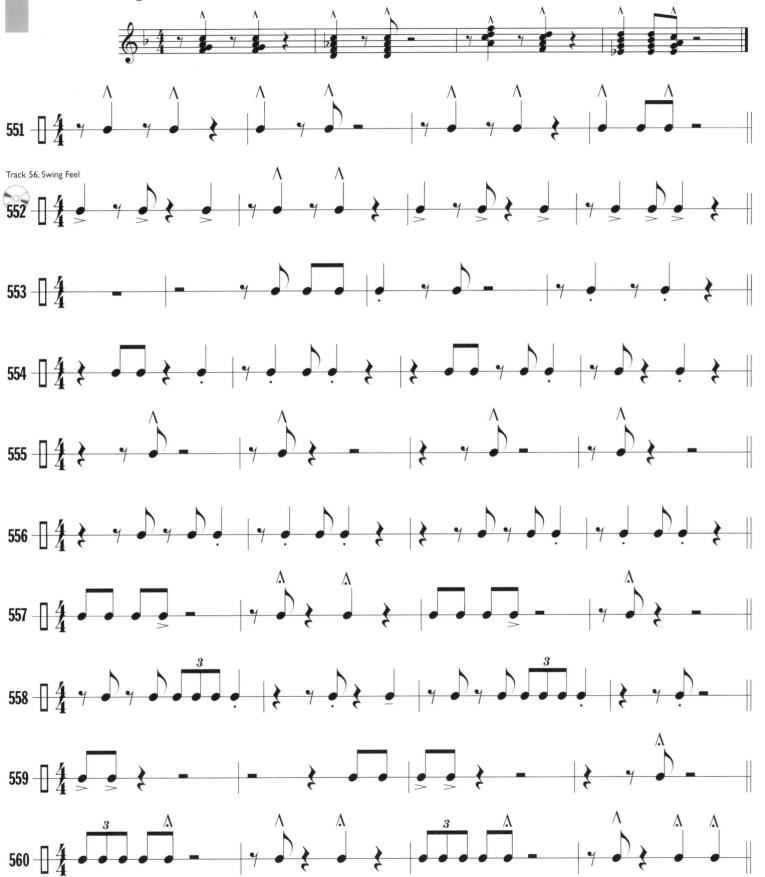

Anticipated 4th Beat & Initial Rests

Exercises 561–570

The following pages deal with the anticipated 4th beat. This shouldn't give you any trouble as it is similar in feel to the anticipated 2nd beat. As always, tap or click for rests on rhythms such as in Exercises 568–570. Exercise 568 might be used as a brass punctuation like this.

Anticipated 4th Beat & Ties Over the Barline

Exercises 571–580

Don't forget to tap or click in appropriate places. This is especially important where long initial rests are combined with long, held notes tied over the barline, as in Ex. 575.

Track 58.1, Swing Feel

Track 58.2, Straight Feel

Anticipated 4th Beat in Staccato Notation

Exercises
581–590

Remember to accent every off-beat eighth note followed by a rest. In Ex. 581, the accents are marked with a > ; in Ex. 582, they are not. Doesn't matter; always accent them, marked or not.

Track 59, Swing Feel

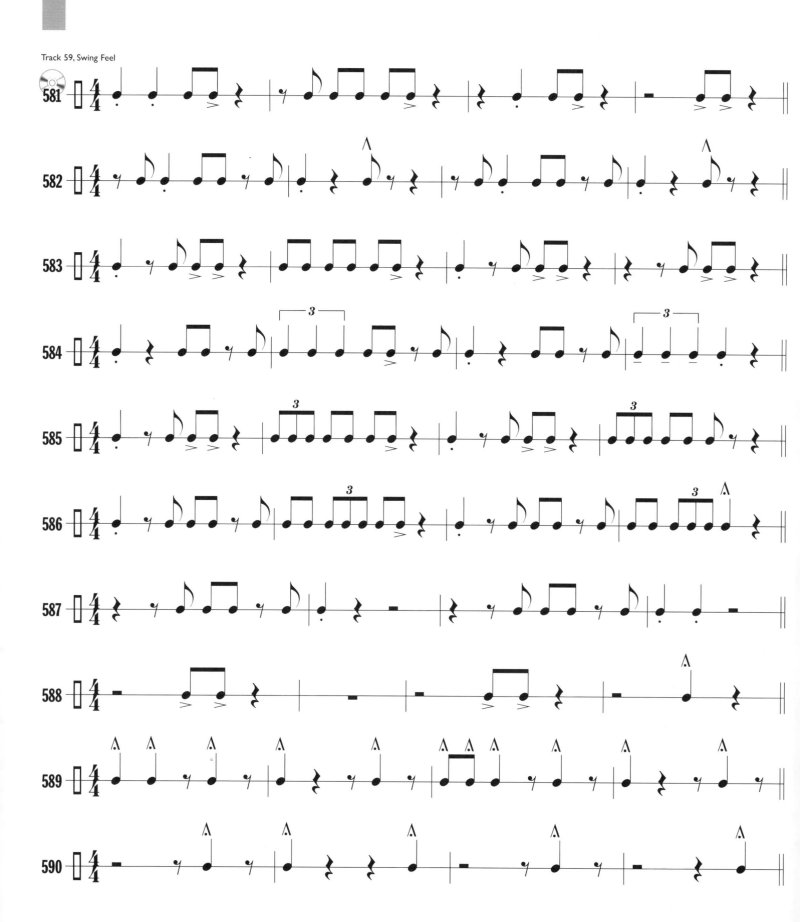

Anticipated 4th or 2nd Beat

Exercises
591–600

These exercises combine the accented 2nd and 4th beats (but not in the same measure). Exercise 599 is a perky little rhythm that could be turned into a melody as below; or make up your own.

Track 60.1, Straight Feel
Track 60.2, Swing Feel

Anticipated 4th or 2nd Beat & Ties Over the Barline

Exercises 601–610

By now, you know the drill. Tap or click for tied notes and for initial rests. Exercises 607 or 609 might be used as background chords for the main melody played by reeds, trombones or even strings. Create melodic fragments out of the other rhythms. For example, Ex. 606 could sound like.

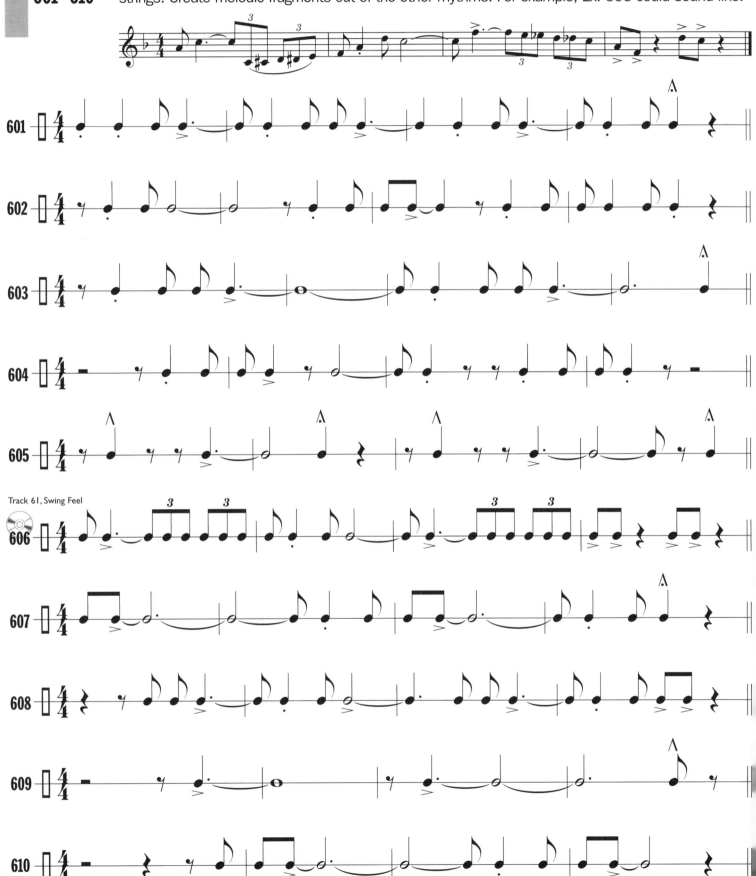

Anticipated 4th or 2nd Beat in Staccato Notation

Exercises 611–620 Most of these figures have been used for brass punctuations or drum breaks. In Ex. 617, the accent and staccato dot mean "short and accented," but not quite as sharply as the "hat" accent and staccato dot (see page 65).

Track 62.1, Straight Feel
Track 62.2, Swing Feel

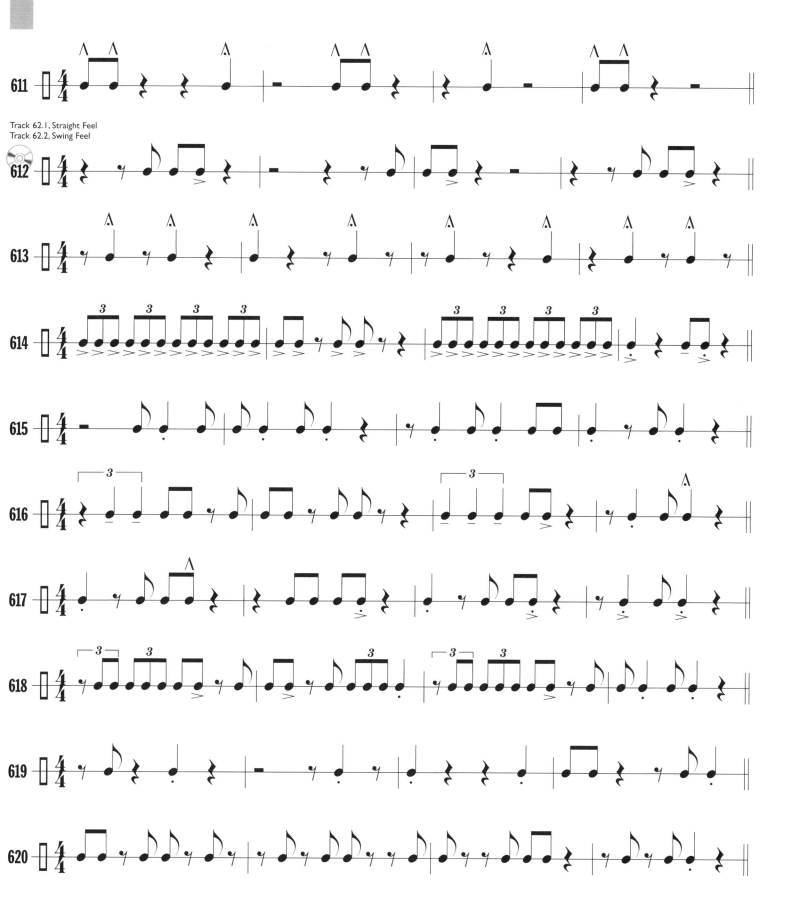

Anticipated 4th, 3rd or 2nd Beat

Exercises **621–630**

So far we've gone through the three easier syncopations, the anticipated 2nd, 3rd, or 4th beat. This page illustrates them all, but never in the same measure.

Track 63.1, Straight Feel
Track 63.2, Swing Feel

Anticipated 4th, 3rd or 2nd Beat & Initial Rests

Exercises
631–640

When playing examples such as Ex. 631, be sure to tap for initial rests. Because the first note is an anticipated 3rd beat, measure 1 requires two taps. Measure 2 requires only one tap, and measure 3 requires three taps.

Track 64, Swing Feel

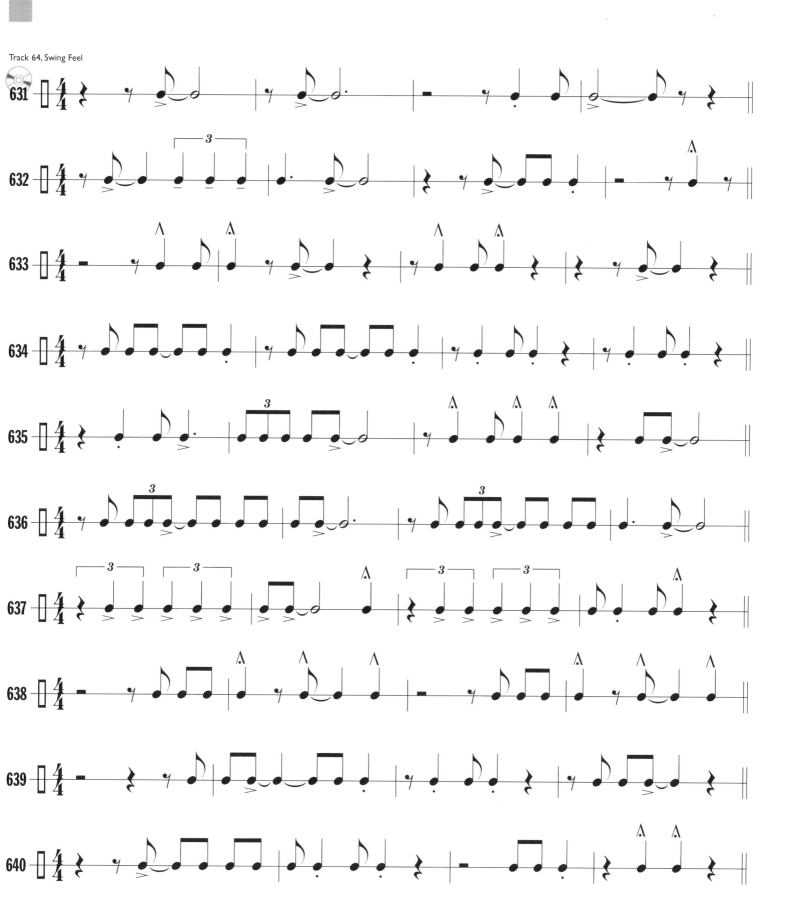

Anticipated 4th, 3rd or 2nd Beat & Ties Over the Barline

Exercises
641–650

If you're using an electronic metronome, as we strongly recommend, make sure it's set to accent the first beat of every group of four. This will help you keep track as you play the exercises on this page, especially those like Exercises 641, 645 and others that use long held notes combined with syncopations. Also, don't forget to tap when the exercise begins with one or more rests.

Track 65.1, Straight Feel
Track 65.2, Swing Feel

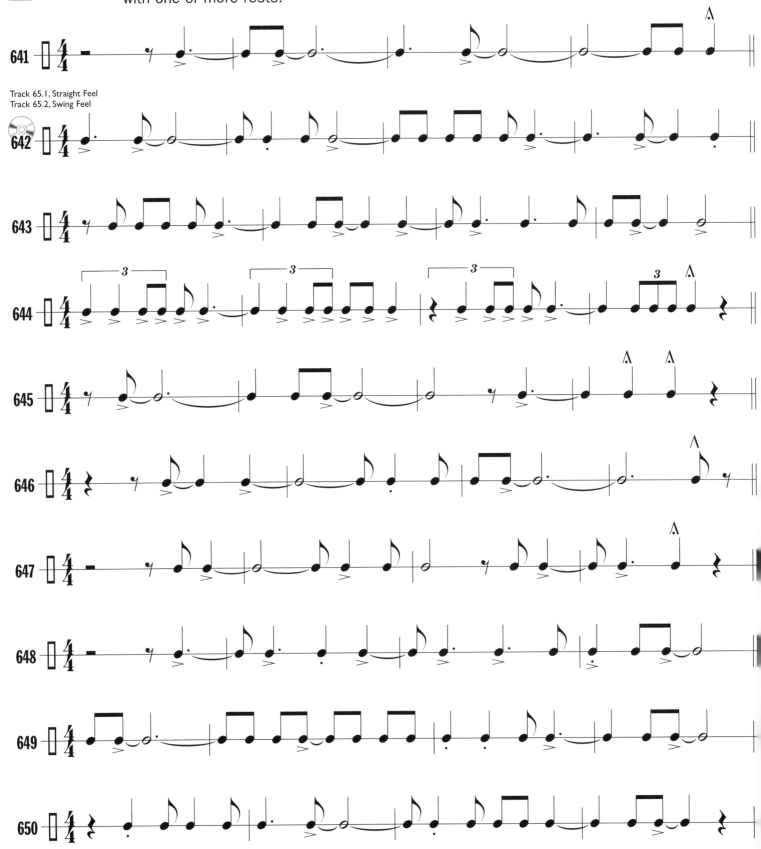

Anticipated 4th, 3rd or 2nd Beat in Staccato Notation

Exercises
651–660

Most of the figures on this page are typical of brass punctuations. Here's how Ex. 658 might be used to punctuate a sax melody.

Exercises 655 and 657 could be used in drum breaks (short solos).

Anticipated 1st Beat

Exercises 661-670

This is the single most difficult syncopation to play correctly because the anticipated note appears in the previous measure. For example, in measure 1 of Ex. 661, the last eighth note is actually the anticipated downbeat of measure 2. If you wish to sing the rhythm, try it this way.

Anticipated 1st Beat & Initial Rests

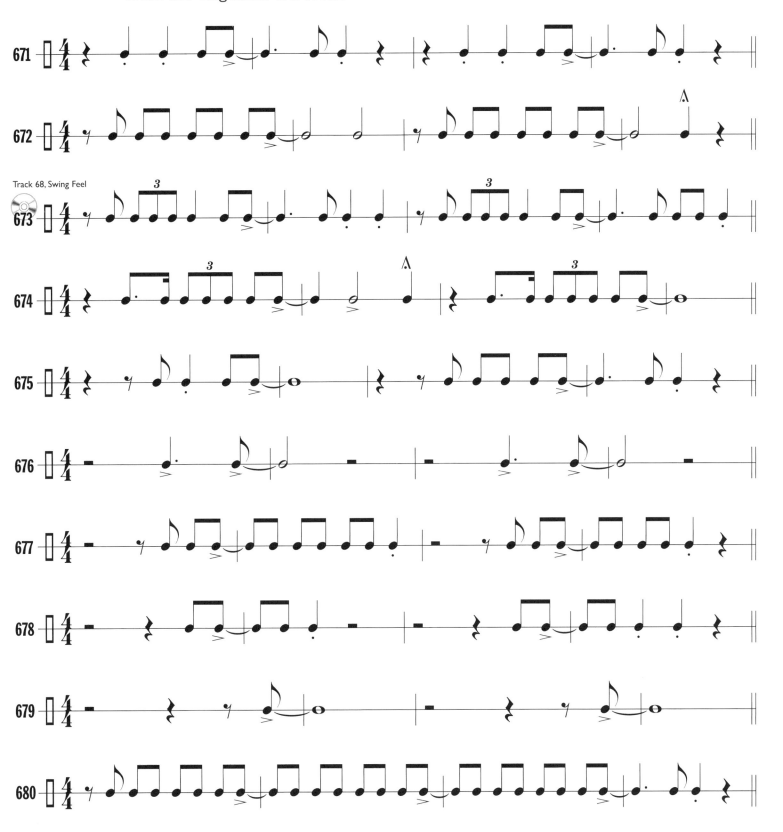

Exercises
671–680

The initial rest increases the complexity, but a foot tap or tongue click will help you keep track. Notice that in measure 2 of Ex. 671, the foot tap is on the 2nd, not the 1st, beat.

Tapping is exceptionally important when playing exercises such as 676–679, which use long notes and rests.

Track 68, Swing Feel

Anticipated 1st Beat & Ties Over the Barline

Exercises
681–690

Whenever the last note of an eighth-note or quarter-note triplet is tied over the barline, it must be accented, as in Exercises 684, 685 and 689. Arrangers sometimes leave out the accents, but a good player will restore them.

Anticipated 1st Beat in Staccato Notation

Exercises 691–700

In staccato notation, the anticipated 1st beat is even more confusing. Since the tied note is omitted, the single eighth note seems to stand alone. Keep in mind, however, that it is still the anticipated first beat of the next measure and should be accented.

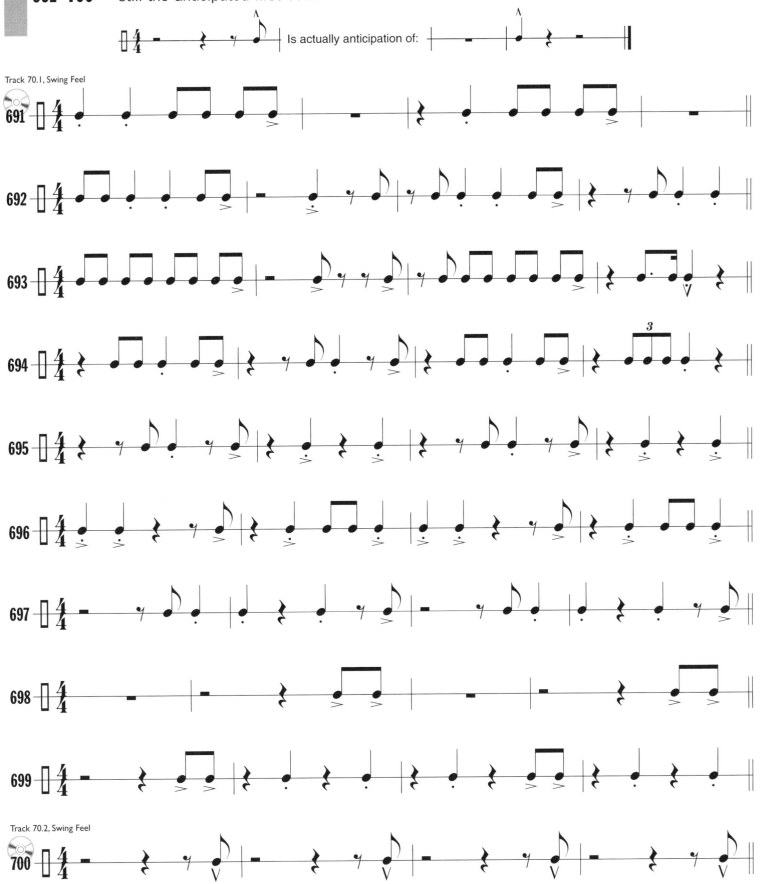

Track 70.1, Swing Feel

Track 70.2, Swing Feel

Anticipated 1st, 2nd, 3rd or 4th Beat

Exercises 701–710

This page reviews all the anticipated notes that are possible in 4/4 time, but never in the same measure. Use the techniques you have already learned.

Track 71, Swing Feel

Anticipated 1st, 2nd, 3rd or 4th Beat & Initial Rests

Exercises
711–720

More review. Use foot taps to ensure proper entrances. Try creating your own melodic version of some or all of these exercises. Here's one possibility based on Ex. 718.

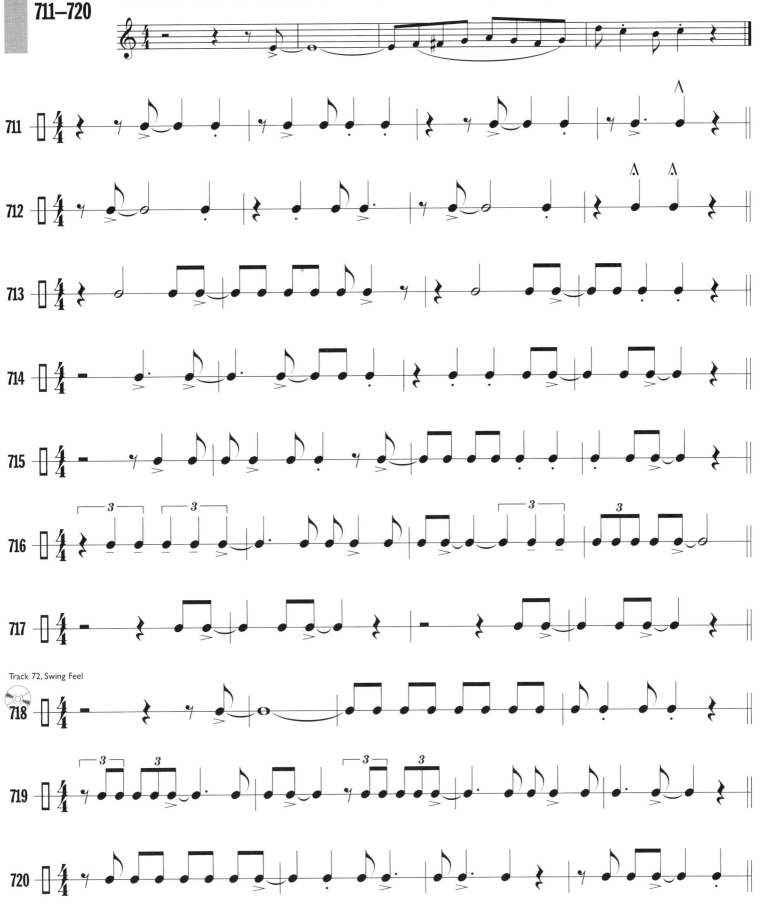

Track 72, Swing Feel

Anticipated 1st, 2nd, 3rd or 4th Beat & Ties Over the Barline

Exercises

721–730 Still more review. Use foot taps to help you keep track of the beat when dealing with ties over the barline.

Track 73, Swing Feel

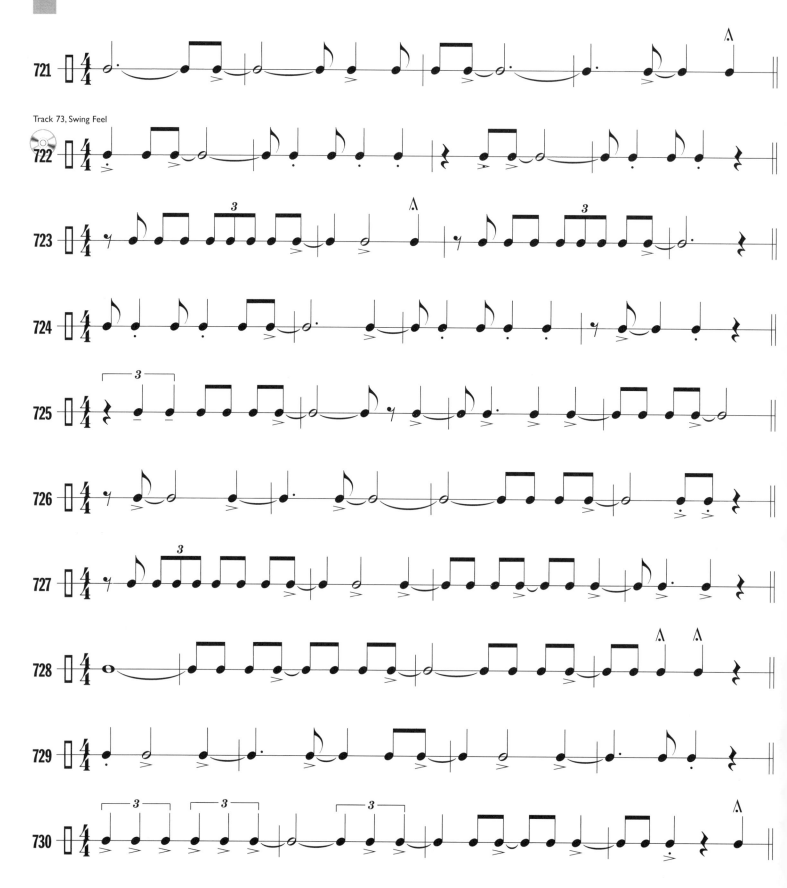

Anticipated 1st, 2nd, 3rd or 4th Beat in Staccato Notation

Exercises 731–740

You may want to review the notes to page 83 before tackling this page. The last few exercises are typical brass punctuations. Here's one version of Ex. 740 punctuating a sax line above.

Track 74, Swing Feel

PART THREE : Double, Triple and Quadruple Syncopations

Of course, modern arrangers don't care how many syncopations there are in a measure. In 4/4 time, you can have as many as four anticipated notes in a single measure, so the syncopations you'll find in this section are all common in today's writing. All the techniques you've learned so far can and should be used to play these figures accurately.

There are a limited number of combinations possible.

Double Syncopations

Two anticipated notes per measure may be

- the 1st and 2nd beats
- the 1st and 3rd beats
- the 1st and 4th beats
- the 2nd and 3rd beats
- the 2nd and 4th beats
- the 3rd and 4th beats

Triple Syncopations

Three anticipations per measure may be

- the 2nd, 3rd and 4th beats

- the 1st, 2nd and 3rd beats

- the 1st, 2nd and 4th beats

- the 1st, 3rd and 4th beats

Quadruple Syncopations

When all four notes are anticipated, there's only one way to do it.

Syncopation and Latin-American Music

Even as far back as the early 1900s, Latin music had an impact on American popular styles. The *tango* developed in the slums of Buenos Aires around the 1880s. Its characteristic rhythm ($\frac{2}{4}$ ♩. ♩ ♫) was an outgrowth of the earlier *habañera*[1], which, as the name suggests, developed in Havana, Cuba. Jelly Roll Morton often spoke of the "Spanish tinge" in his music. Since this jazz piano pioneer developed his style in cosmopolitan New Orleans, it's not surprising that he was familiar with various Caribbean and South American rhythms and incorporated them in his playing. A development of the tango rhythm ($\frac{4}{4}$ ♪ ♩ ♪ ♩ ♩) can be found in the second strain[2] of "St. Louis Blues" (1914), where it creates a welcome contrast to the four-to-the-bar rhythms of the first and third strains.

Both the *rhumba* and the *beguine* became popular in the late 1920s after they were introduced to American audiences by the Xavier Cugat Orchestra. But it was after World War II that Latin music came into its own and became an everyday part of the musical scene. Many dances and the music that went with them, including the *conga, cha-cha-cha, merengue,* and *mambo,* washed over American music and then receded, leaving permanent traces, especially rhythmically. Like jazz, Latin music is highly syncopated, but unlike the swing feeling of jazz, the upbeat eighth notes of Latin music are played exactly as long as the downbeats.

Most Latin music is based on the so-called clave (pronounced CLAH-vay) beat ($\frac{4}{4}$ ♩. ♪ ♩ ♩ | ♪ ♩ ♩ ♪) which is itself syncopated. Claves are two hollow sticks which, when struck together, produce a penetrating click that permeates the ensemble. It is the foundation of the Latin-American band.

In the 1960s the Brazilian *bossa nova* brought a new harmonic sophistication to Latin music. It soon became very popular with American jazz musicians and remains so today. The *bossa* makes a subtle, but very important, modification to the clave beat, increasing the amount of syncopation in the music ($\frac{4}{4}$ ♩. ♪ ♩ ♩ | ♪ ♩ ♪ ♩.).

Salsa is a combination of American jazz harmonies and melodies and Latin rhythms. The underlying rhythm is usually based on the clave beat, but melodically the eighth notes are played with a swing, not a straight, feel.

Today the Latin influence on American music is stronger than ever, The latest import is an exciting sound from Mexico called *tejano* (teh-HA-no). It is, however, not based on the clave beat but derives from the accordion based polkas which German immigrants brought with them to Mexico in the 19th century.

---

[1] The most famous example of a habañera is the one from the opera "Carmen," inadvertently plagiarized by Bizet from a piece written 20 years before by Spanish composer Sebastian Yradier. Bizet apparently thought it was a folk song.

[2] The second strain begins with the words "St. Louis woman, with her diamond rings . . ."

Anticipated 2nd & 4th Beat

Exercises 741–750

When playing with the swing feel, anticipated 2nd and 4th beats are almost always cut off short, see Ex. 741 below. On this page we have been careful to indicate this by using a staccato dot, but the meticulous player will do this even when not indicated in the notation.

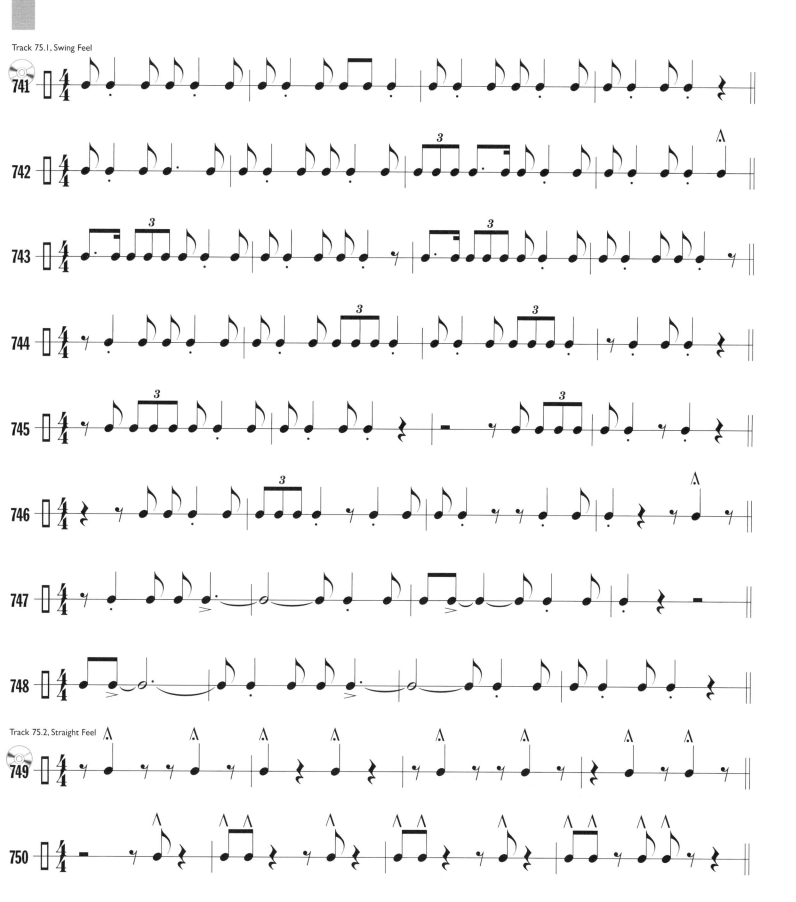

Anticipated 2nd & 3rd Beat

Exercises 751–760

As stated on the previous page, most anticipated 2nd beats are cut off short by the swing player. For example, measure 1 of Ex. 751 is written:

but usually played:

Track 76.1, Straight Feel
Track 76.2, Swing Feel

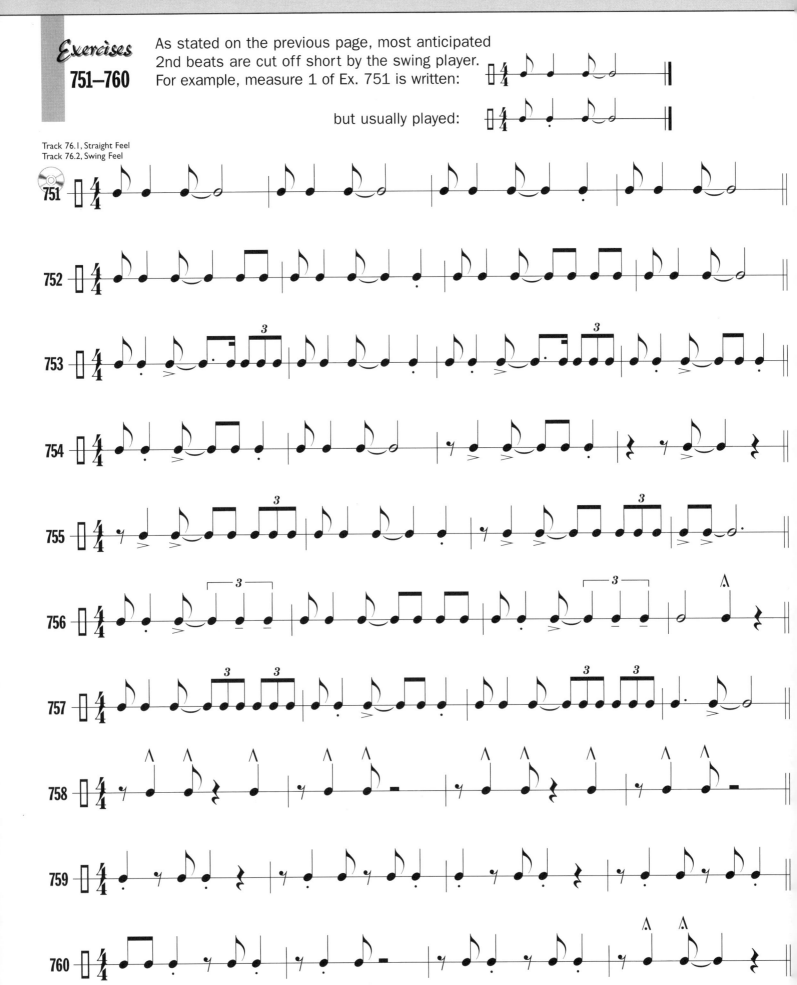

Anticipated 3rd & 4th Beat

Exercises
761–770

As indicated earlier, the anticipated 4th beat is usually cut off short in the swing feel. But in Ex. 761, measure 1, it's probably the anticipated 3rd beat that would be cut off short.

Track 77.1, Straight Feel
Track 77.2, Swing Feel

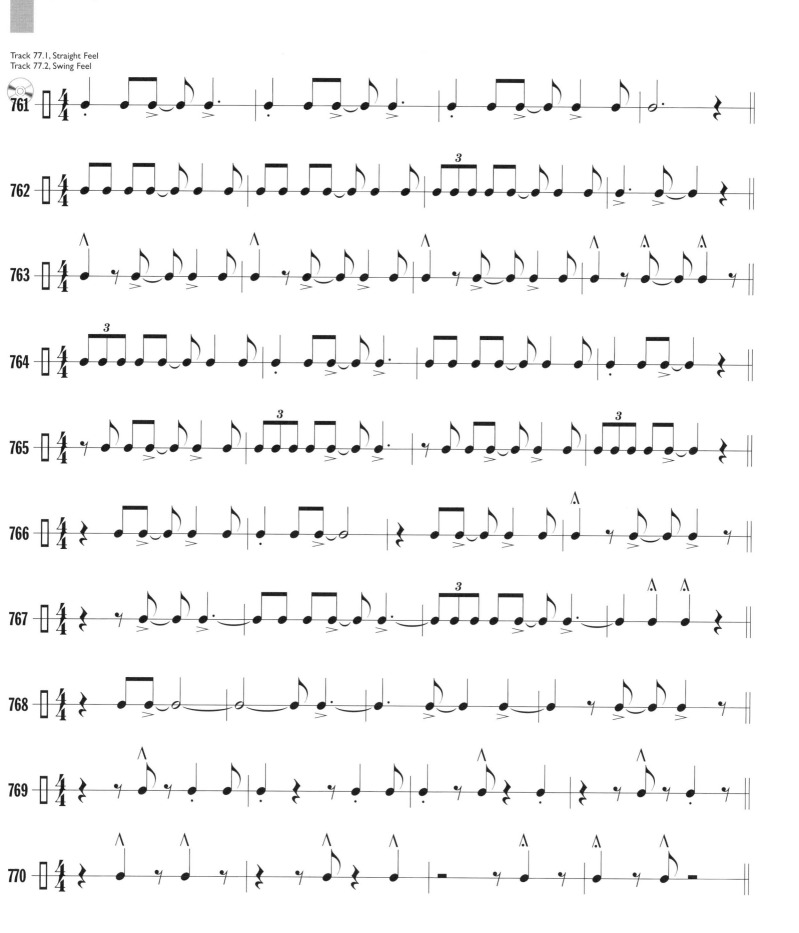

Anticipated 1st & 2nd Beat

Exercises 771–780

If the anticipated 2nd beat is tied to a longer note such as in Ex. 771, measures 1 and 3, it isn't cut off short; in measures 2 and 4, it is. Work especially hard on this whole page because the anticipated 1st beat is used frequently in modern arrangements. It's an important means of giving the music "drive."

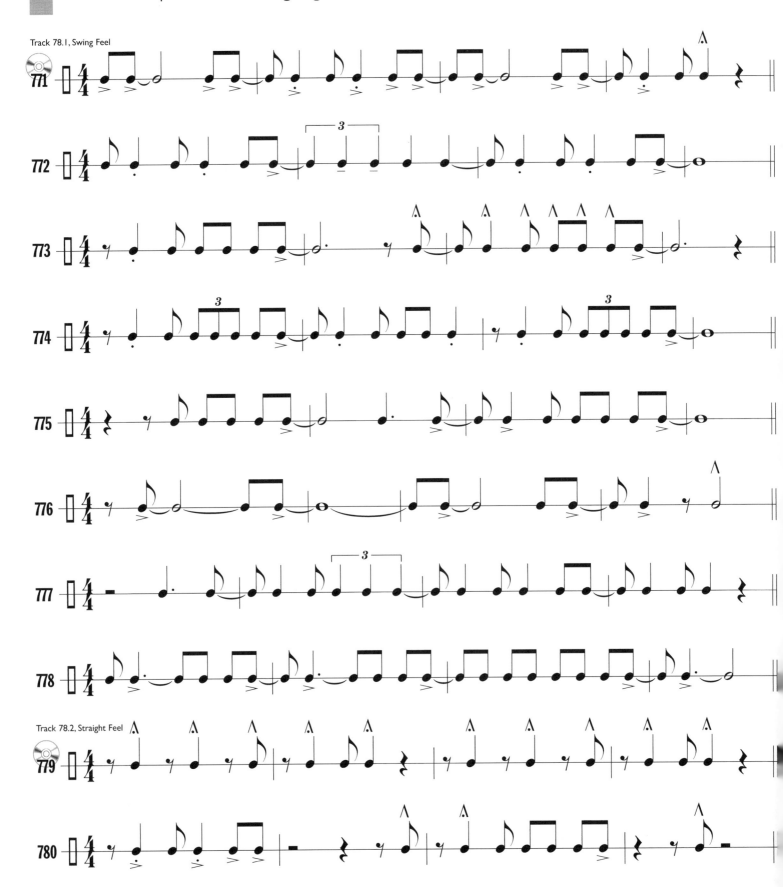

Track 78.1, Swing Feel

Track 78.2, Straight Feel

Anticipated 1st & 3rd Beat

Exercises 781–790

You can create your own melodies using Exercises 781–787. The last three exercises are more likely to be used for brass punctuations or comping figures for guitar or piano.

Track 79.1, Swing Feel

Track 79.2, Straight Feel

Anticipated 1st & 4th Beat

Exercises
791–800

You could construct a typical Las Vegas-style "show biz" fanfare from Exercise 793. Exercise 799 could be used for brass punctuations or piano or guitar comping.

Anticipated 2nd, 3rd & 4th Beat

Exercises 801–810

This page explores triple syncopations, sometimes with quarter notes and eighth notes, sometimes with triplets. Either way, if you're playing with a swing feel, your approach should be the same. Especially watch your counting in Ex. 807, where a very long note is contrasted with a syncopated figure.

Track 81.1, Swing Feel

Track 81.2, Straight Feel

Anticipated 1st, 2nd & 3rd Beat

Exercises
811–820

Try constructing melodies from Exercises 811–815. Exercises 816–820 are more likely to be used as brass or sax punctuations, or comping patterns for guitar or keyboard.

Anticipated 1st, 2nd & 4th Beat

Exercises **821–830**

Notice the last half of measure 3 in Ex. 828.

This figure: [music notation] is often written: [music notation]

There is no difference in the playing of these two figures.

Track 83.1, Swing Feel

Track 83.2, Straight Feel

Anticipated 1st, 3rd & 4th Beat

Exercises 831–840

Highly syncopated figures like the ones in this section are characteristic of many kinds of Latin-American music. The proper feel places the anticipated notes squarely on the upbeat, the way a classical musician would play them. The major exception to this rule is Latin music that has been influenced by American jazz and swing, such as salsa. Salsa brass and reed players tend to interpret eighth notes and syncopations with a swing feel while the rhythm section plays with a straight feel.

Track 84.1, Straight Feel

Track 84.2, Swing Feel

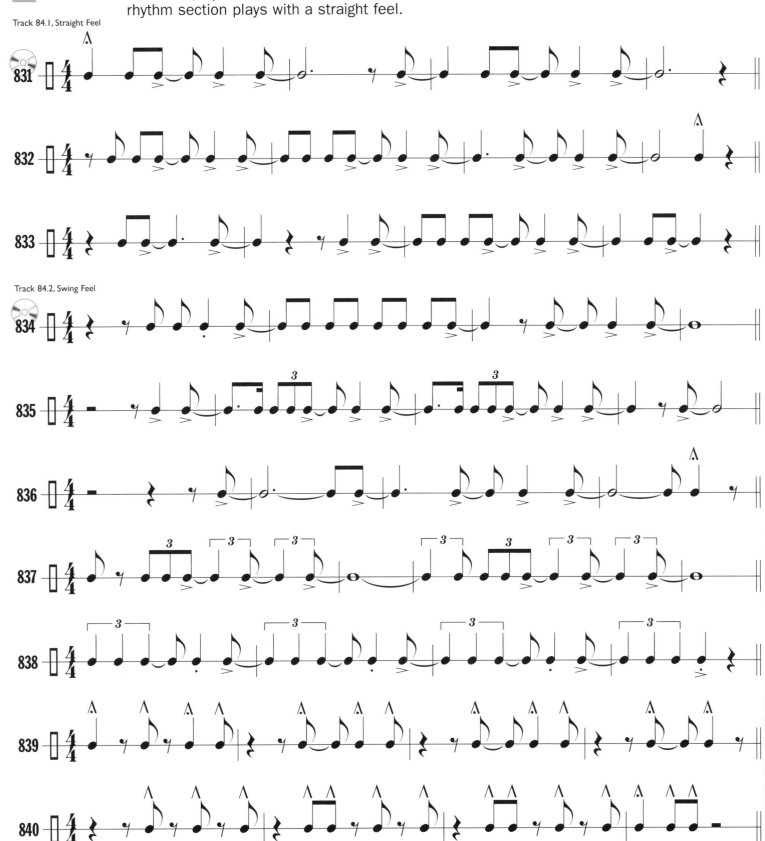

Anticipated 1st, 2nd, 3rd & 4th Beat

Exercises
841–850

This page presents the ultimate in 4/4 time syncopation. Please note that in measure 2 of Ex. 841 and other places, when an anticipated quarter note occurs over the middle of the measure, it is written as two eighth notes tied together. This is so the middle of the measure is shown clearly. Except for obvious rhythms such as:

Every measure of 4/4 should be written so it can be broken into two measures of 2/4.

Track 85, Swing Feel

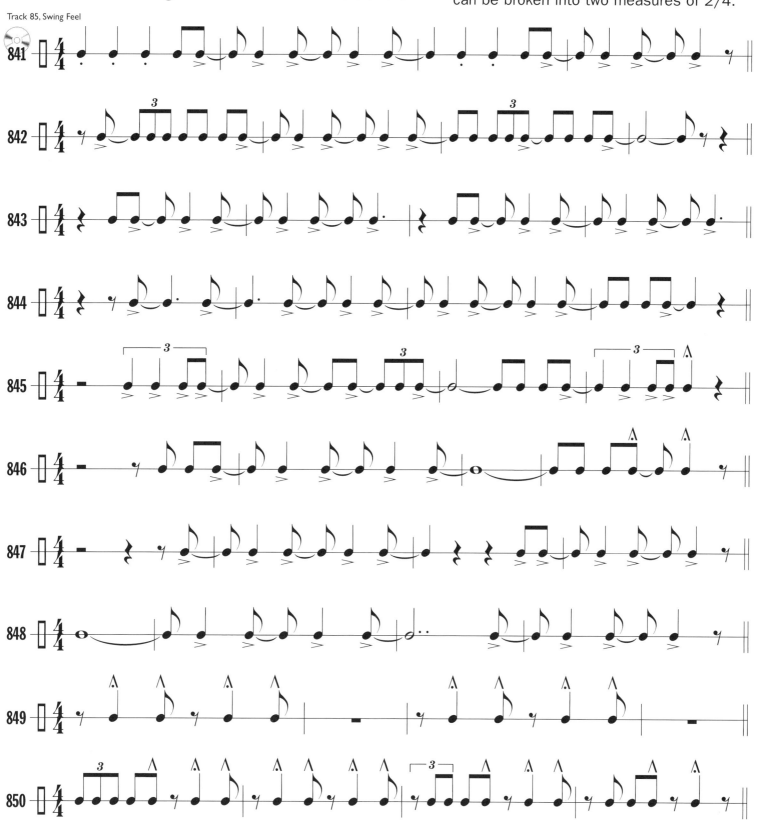

PART FOUR : *Syncopated Accents*

Strictly speaking, off-beat accents are not syncopations or anticipations, but they give a similar effect. The ordinary way of playing, say, eight eighth notes is in pairs of two with each downbeat receiving a slight stress.

By placing accents on offbeats, it's possible to obtain a syncopated effect. This was one of the earliest techniques used in jazz and swing as this excerpt from "Twelfth Street Rag" [1912] shows.

You can practice several ways. If you're using rhythm syllables, make sure to say those below the accented notes louder.

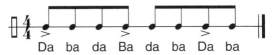

Da   ba   da   Ba   da   ba   Da   ba

Another way to practice is to play swing eighth notes with one hand and accent with the other.

Right hand

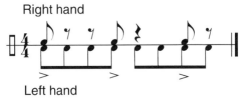

Left hand

This is typical drum technique, but is valuable for any instrumentalist.

Syncopations in Cut-Time (alla breve)

The symbol for cut time (or alla breve) is ¢ or 2/2. It means that the measure (which contains the same number of notes as 4/4) is to be counted with two beats to the bar instead of four. The whole note gets two beats, the half note gets one beat, the quarter note gets half a beat, and so on.

1   2   1   2   1   &   2   &   1   uh   &   uh   2   uh   &   uh

Cut time is characteristic of many different styles, including 1920s fox trots, some marches, most Dixieland jazz, many Broadway show tunes and Las Vegas style show music. The swing feel is not used in any of these styles, so practice with a straight feel. Here are a few examples:

"Margie" (1920 fox trot)

Brightly

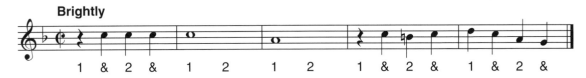

1   &   2   &   1   2   1   2   1   &   2   &   1   &   2   &

"Colonel Bogey" (1914 march)

March tempo

1 & 2 & 1 & 2 & 1 & 2 & 1 & 2 &

"Back Home Again in Indiana" (1917 Dixieland standard)

Bright Dixie feel

1 & 2 & 1 2 1 & 2 & 1 2

Counting in cut time, even if the piece is written in 4/4, is a valuable technique to use when the tempo gets fast. Trying to tap your foot four to the bar when the time is flying by at, say, 200 beats per minute, is an almost guaranteed way to start dragging the beat or losing your place. After mastering the basics of playing in cut time, we recommend reviewing the earlier exercises at faster tempos, counting in two.

Double-Time Syncopation in $\frac{2}{4}$($\frac{4}{4}$)

Starting in the 1960s, a new rhythmic element entered American rock music, the so-called "boogaloo beat." This consists of an eight-to-the-bar rhythmic feel; that is, rather than the quarter note being the basic rhythmic unit, the eighth note becomes primary. A typical example of this feel is The Beatles' "Let It Be" or The BeeGees' "Stayin' Alive."

The exercises on pages 108–114 are written so they can be played in 4/4 time using only the solid bar lines. Virtually all double-time rock is notated this way. Alternatively, using both the solid and dotted barlines, they can be played in 2/4. Most tangos and many early ragtime pieces are written in 2/4.

You'll find that these double-time figures actually sound the same as the 4/4 syncopations you have studied on pages 40–100; they are just notated differently. For example, if you play:

with a straight feel, the final result is indistinguishable from:

The swing feel is not used in double time, so practice these exercises only with the straight feel.

Eighth Notes with Offbeat Accents

Anticipated 1st & 2nd Beat

Exercises
861–870

Count two to the bar and create some melodies of your own. Ex. 861 might be played:

(As a matter of fact, the rhythm is similar to Cole Porter's "Another Opening, Another Show.")

Exercise 863 may suggest a tune that amateur pianists play on the black keys, "Georgie Porgie." The half note triplets in Ex. 866 may suggest parts of Porter's "I Get a Kick Out of You" or Jule Styne's "Ev'rything's Comin' Up Roses."

Track 86.3 Straight Feel

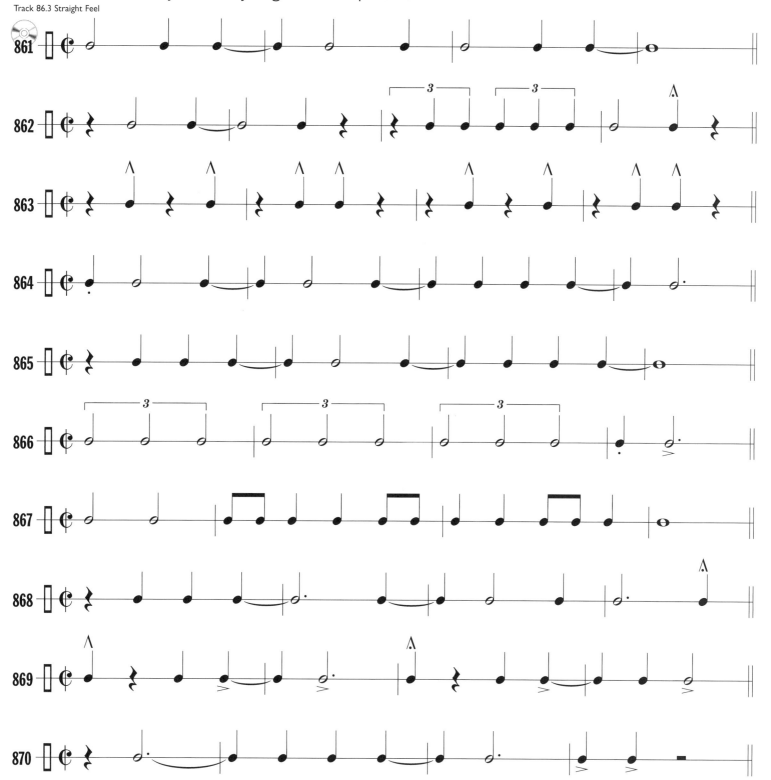

Anticipated 1st & 2nd Beat with Variations

Exercises 871–880 More exercises in cut time. If you're using an electronic metronome, don't forget to set it for two beats to the bar with the first beat accented. Exercise 872 may remind you of the 1950s doo-wop classic "My Prayer."

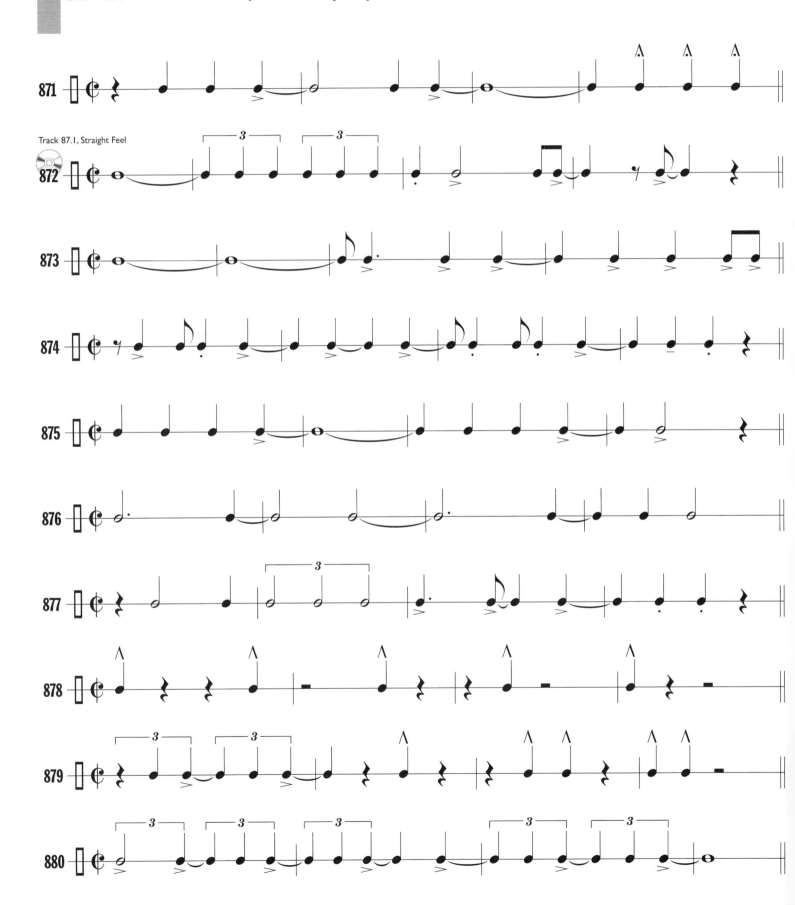

2/4 or 4/4 Time

Exercises
881–890

The disco craze of the 1970s was heavily dependent on double-time rhythms. Exercise 881 is identical to the opening measures of the disco anthem "The Hustle." The figure in Ex. 882 plays a prominent role in George Harrison's "Something" and has also been used in many other tunes.

Track 87.2, Straight Feel

Track 87.3, Straight Feel

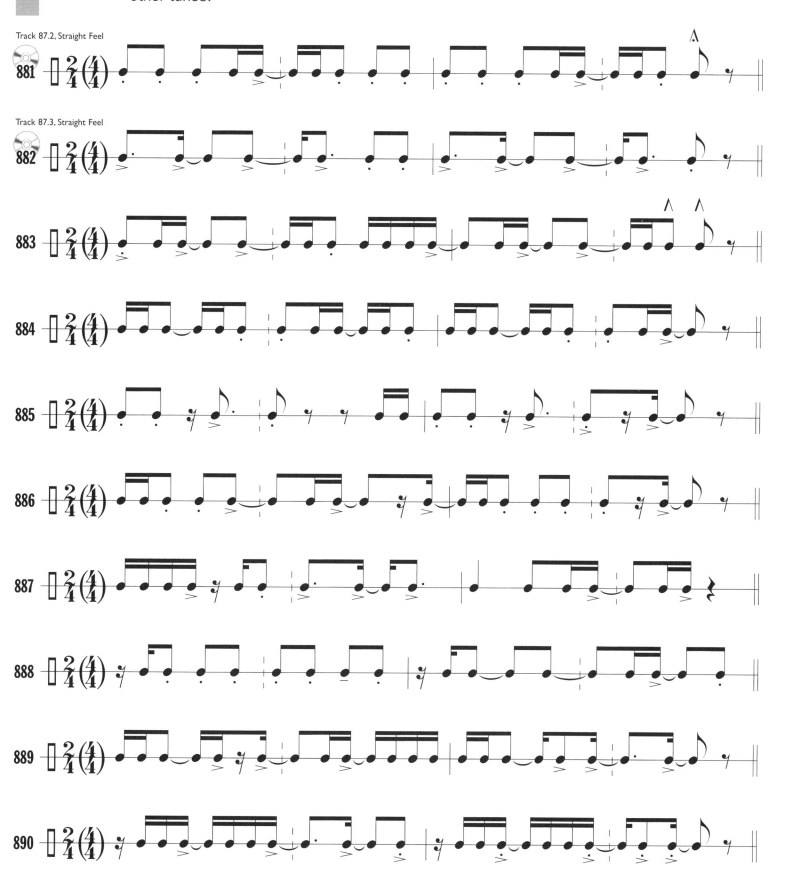

2/4 or 4/4 Time (cont.)

Exercises 891–900

If Ex. 893 were shifted one beat earlier, it would bear more than a passing resemblance to the "Rocky" theme. Exercises 898 and 899 are double-time versions of the off-beat accents explored on page 104.

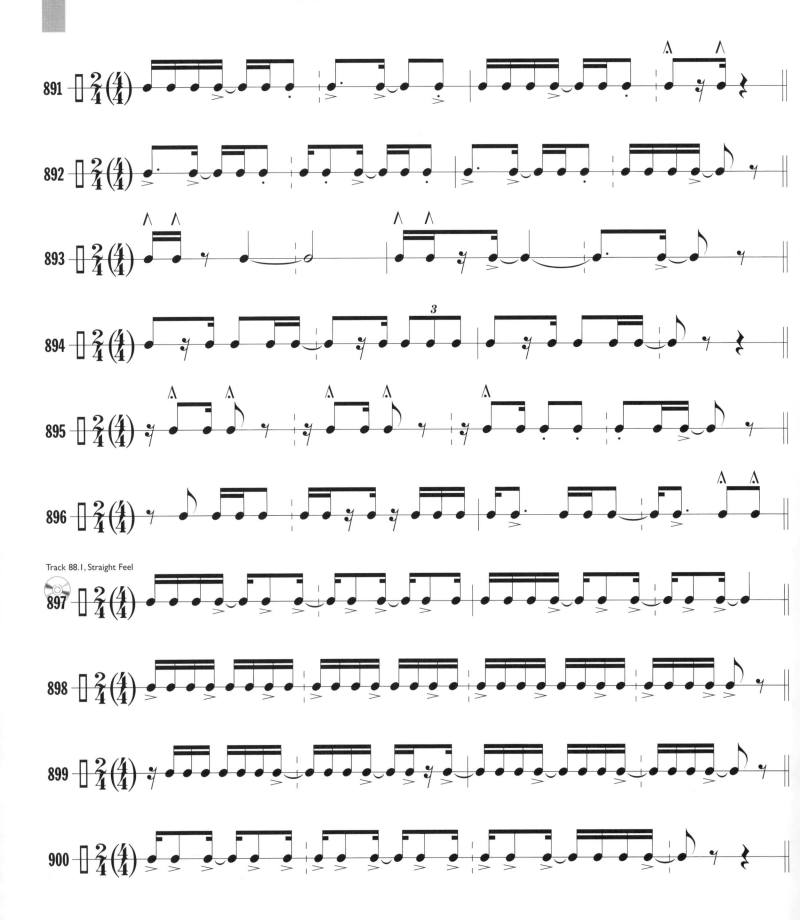

2/4 or 4/4 Time (cont.)

Exercises
901–910

Exercise 901 might be found in a boogaloo-style piece as:

Exercise 902 contains a rhythm used in a famous Led Zeppelin song, "Kashmir." The two 16th plus eighth note figure repeats over and over, but always on a different beat. Exercises 908–910 might be found in any number of tangos.

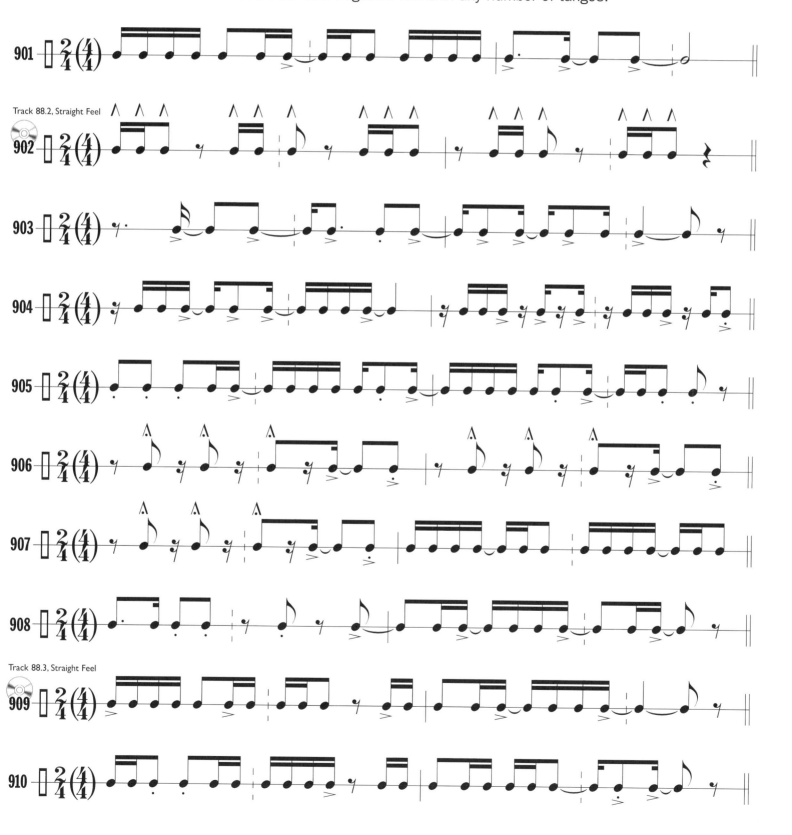

2/4 or 4/4 Time (cont.)

Exercises

911–920

As always, it's trickier to play rests than notes. Be especially careful of Exercises 911, 912 and 914. Don't forget to use the foot tap technique. Ex. 917 could be the bass figure for a rock tune.

Track 89.1, Straight Feel

2/4 or 4/4 Time (cont.)

Exercises

921–930   Don't forget to use foot taps on missing beats
such as in Exercises 921, 922, 924, 925, and 927–930.

Track 89.2, Straight Feel

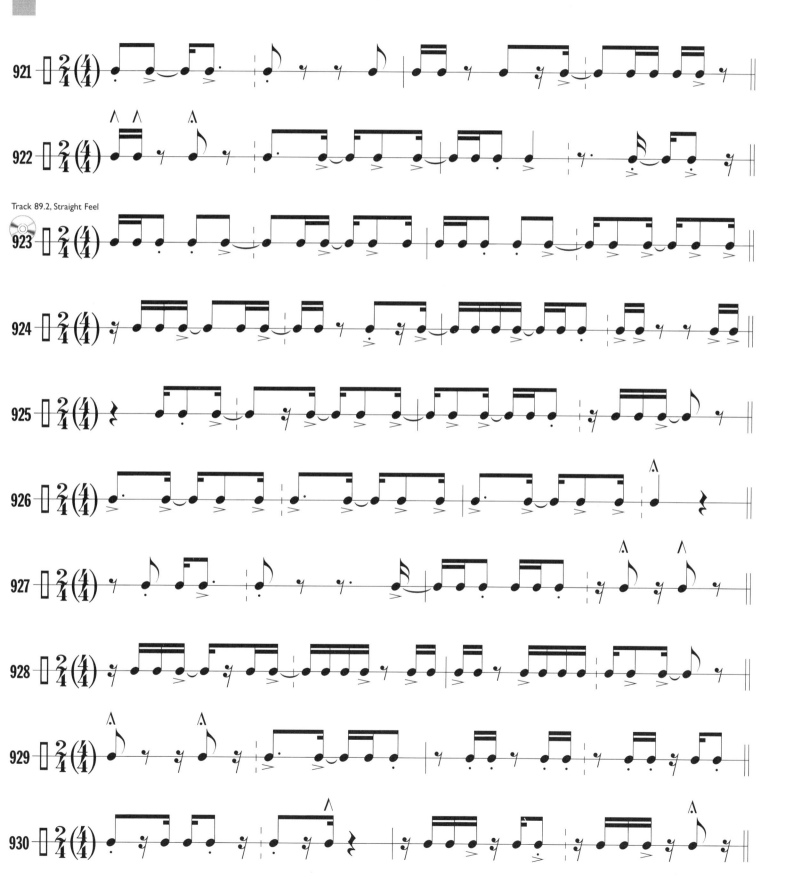

2/4 or 4/4 Time (cont.)

Exercises
931–940

Foot taps are especially important with long notes such as in Ex. 931 and exercises with many rests such as 934 and 935. Many of these figures can be used to construct boogaloo bass lines, such as using Ex. 933 to play:

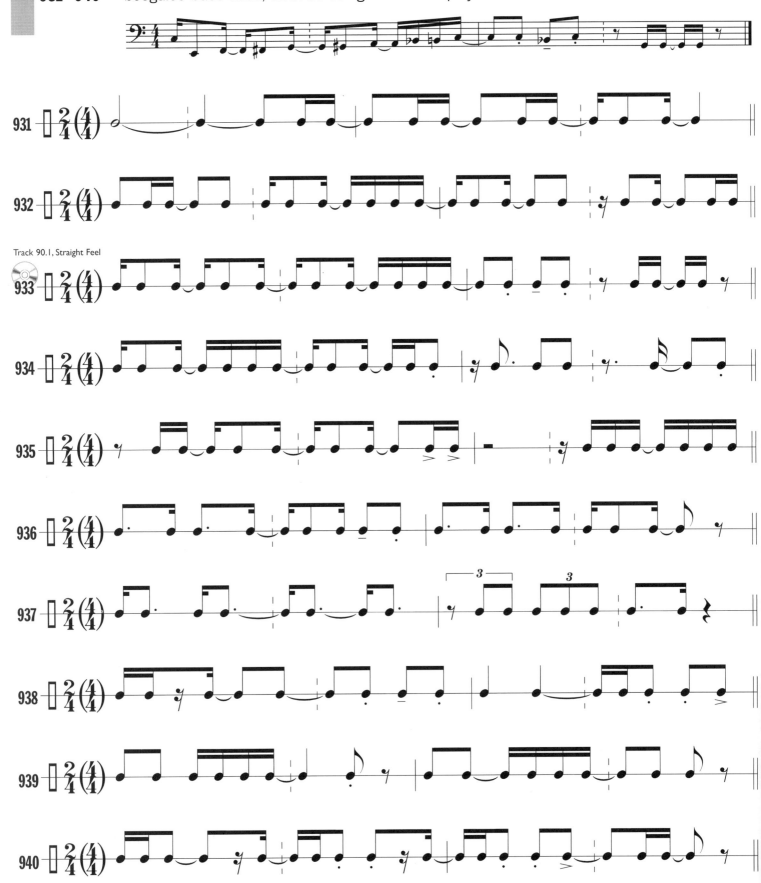

Track 90.1, Straight Feel

2/4 or 4/4 Time (cont.)

Exercises
941–950

Create some sax or brass figures with exercises such as 944.

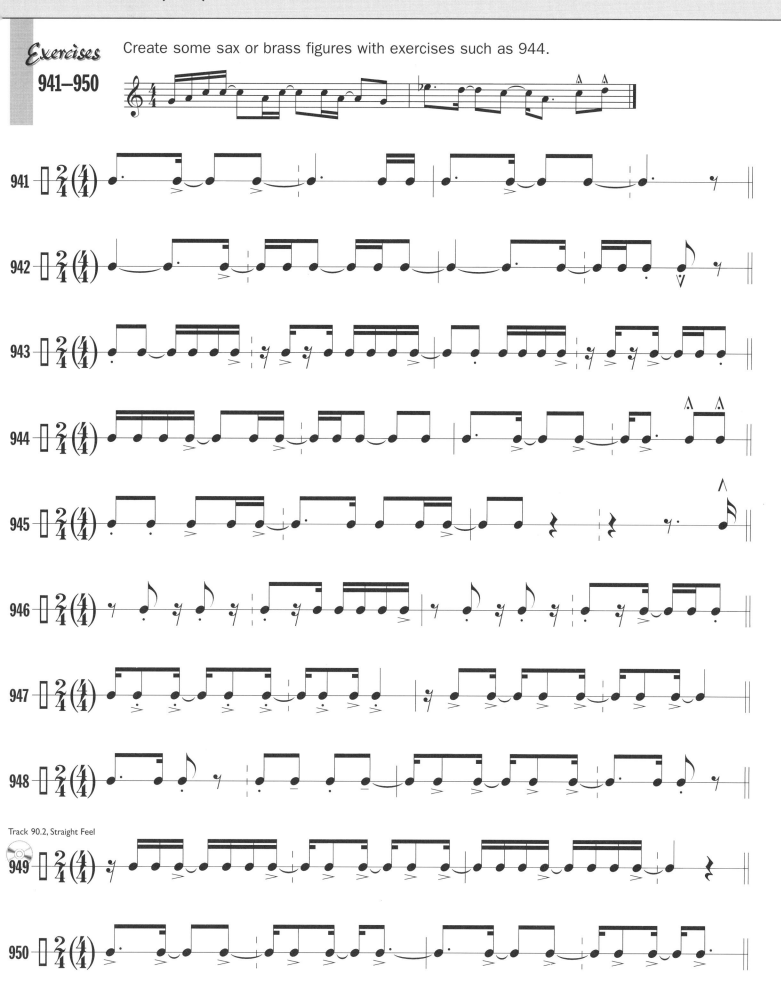

PART FIVE : *Basic Rhythms &*
Syncopations in 3/4 Time

The first four sections in this book are devoted to 4/4 time and its variations, cut time and double-time. This is because probably 95% of what the working musician runs across is in these meters. Nevertheless, the modern player must be familiar with other meters as well.

Foremost of these is 3/4, which is used for waltzes and some avant garde jazz pieces. When 3/4 is played at a slow to moderate tempo it is best to count "in three," that is, one beat for each quarter note.

However, when the beat is fast, as in the Viennese waltzes of Johann Strauss and others, and certain American waltzes like Rodgers and Hart's "Lover," it is better to count "in one," that is, one beat per measure.

Since at first this will be difficult to feel correctly, we suggest starting at a slow to moderate tempo in three (♩ = 80 to about 160) and gradually working your way up to ♩. = 54–60 or faster. The swing feel is not used for waltzes except where specifically called for, e.g., Jerome Kern's "Waltz in Swingtime" or Fats Waller's "Jitterbug Waltz." Nevertheless, some avant garde jazz arrangements do use the swing feel in 3/4, and examples of this are given on pages 119 and 120.

Of course, all the techniques you have learned in this book in 4/4 time, like foot taps or tongue clicks, can and should be used in 3/4 time. This especially applies to notes tied over the bar line and initial rests.

Eighth & Quarter Rests & Ties Over the Barline

Exercises 951–960

Start by practicing these exercises at a slow to moderate tempo and count in three. Gradually increase the speed on your metronome, and when you get to about 160 beats per minute, start feeling each measure as one slow beat, about 54 beats per minute. Then gradually increase this speed to the limit of your technique.

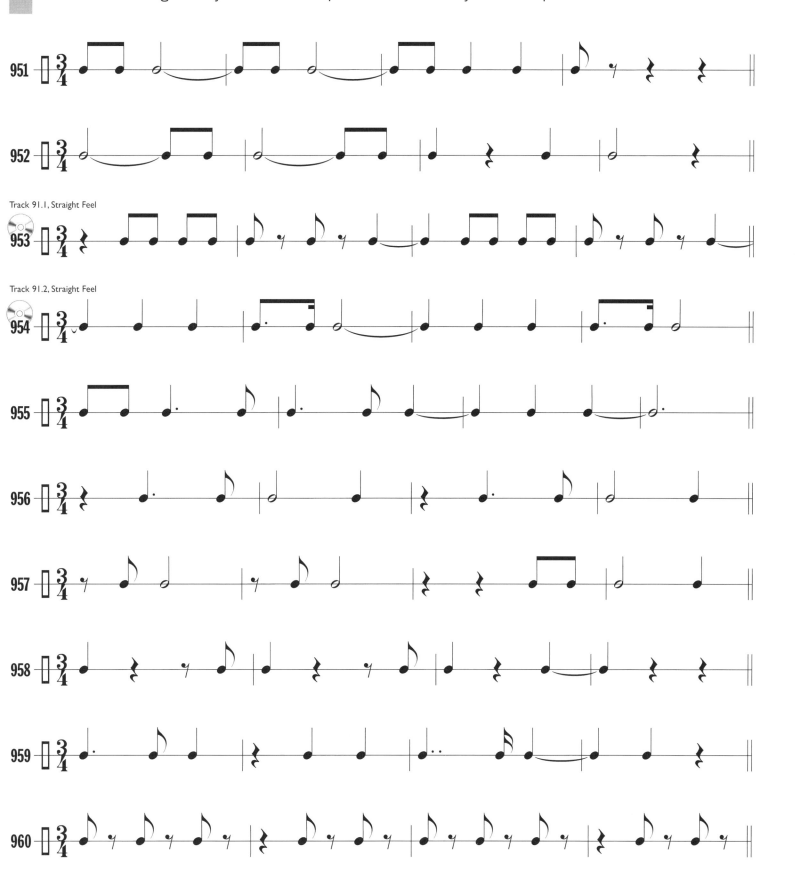

Eighth & Quarter Rests & Ties Over the Barline (cont.)

Exercises **961–970** Don't forget to tap or click for initial rests and notes tied over the barline. Create a waltz based on some or all of these rhythms. For example, Ex. 961 might sound like this.

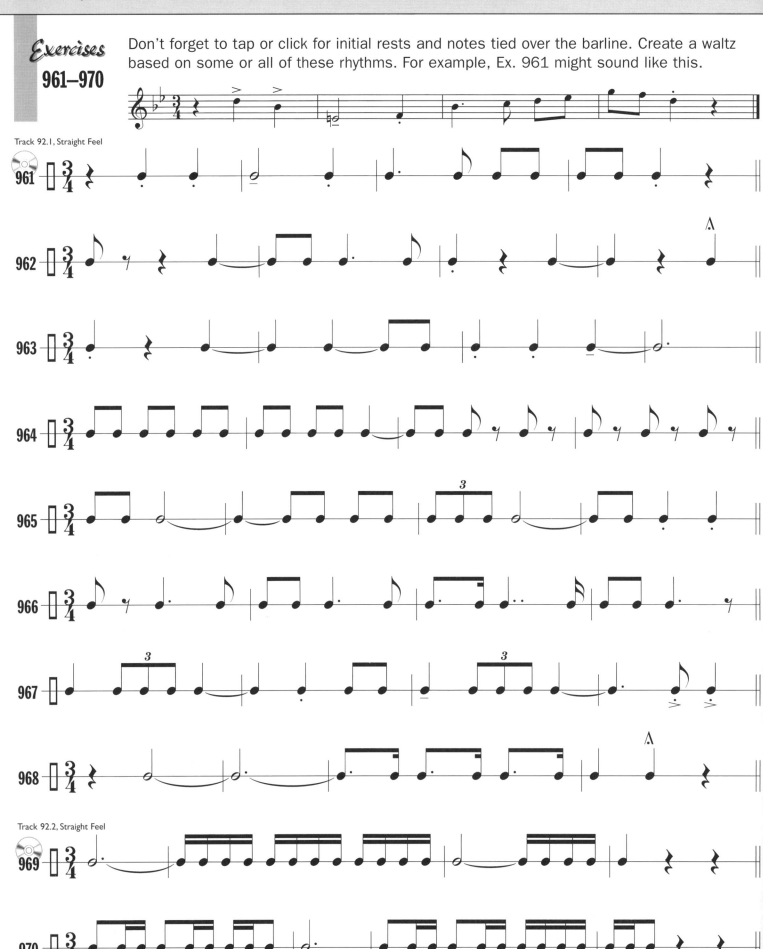

Track 92.1, Straight Feel

Track 92.2, Straight Feel

Hemiolas

Exercises
971–980

A hemiola is a rhythmic figure that fools the ear into thinking it is hearing a figure in a different meter. For example, if you hear:

you might think you are hearing:

Exercises 972–977 are more subtle figures that all sound like three measures of 2/4 rather than two measures of 3/4. This effect can also be achieved by accenting in unusual places such as in Ex. 980, where accenting each group of four eighth notes suggests three measures of 2/4 rather than the written two measures of 3/4. Using hemiolas is one way of adding interest and excitement to pieces in 3/4 time.

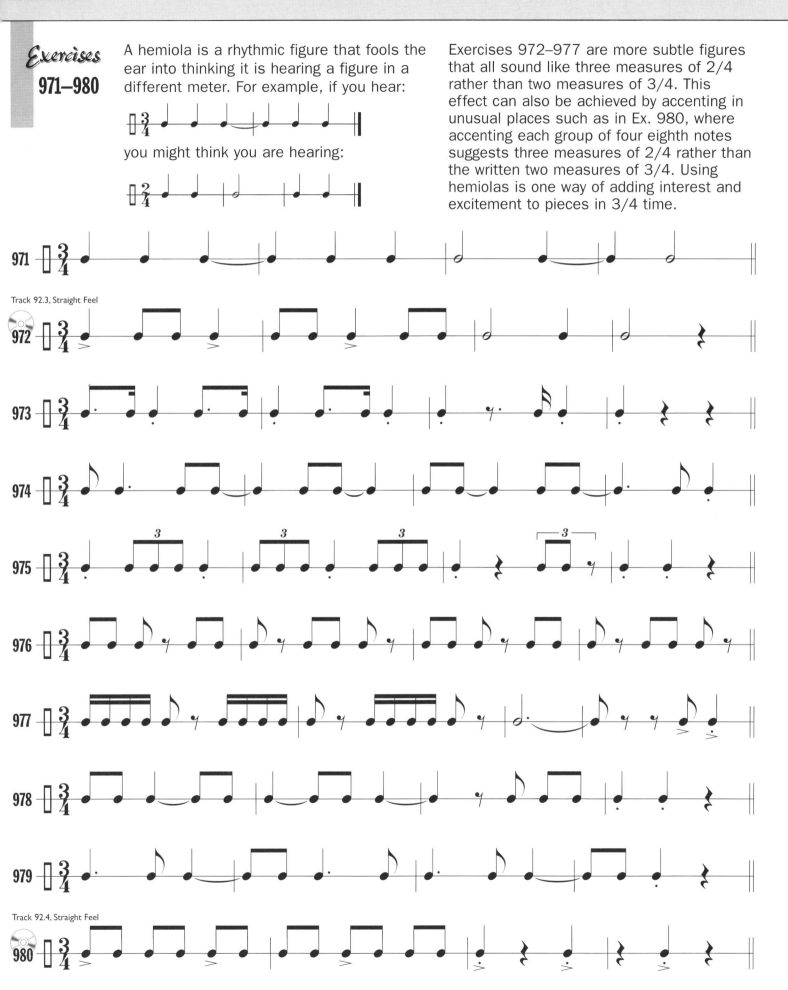

Track 92.3, Straight Feel

Track 92.4, Straight Feel

Various Syncopations with Ties Over the Barline

Exercises
981–990

These exercises are meant to be played with the swing feel. Follow the articulations (accent marks) carefully, and play or sing with an easy swing.

Track 93.1, Swing Feel

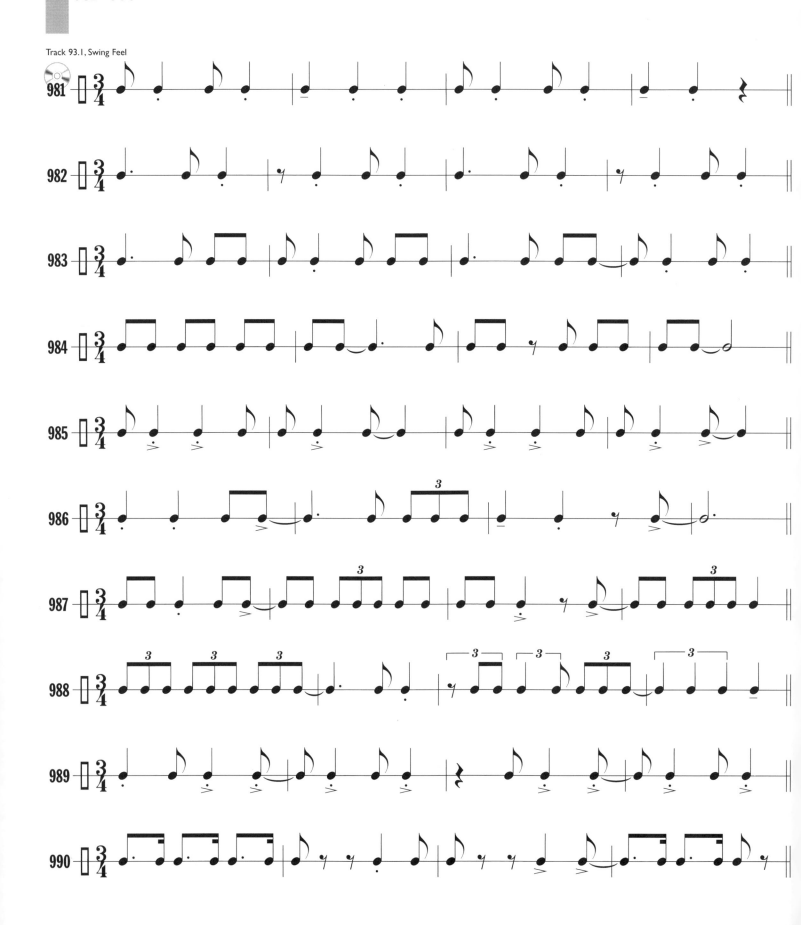

Initial Rests

Exercises 991–1000

Keep the rhythm swinging and make sure to mark the initial rests with foot taps or tongue clicks, one in Exercises 991, 992, 996, 998 and 999; two in Exercises 993, 994, 997 and 1000; three in Ex. 995.

Track 93.2, Swing Feel

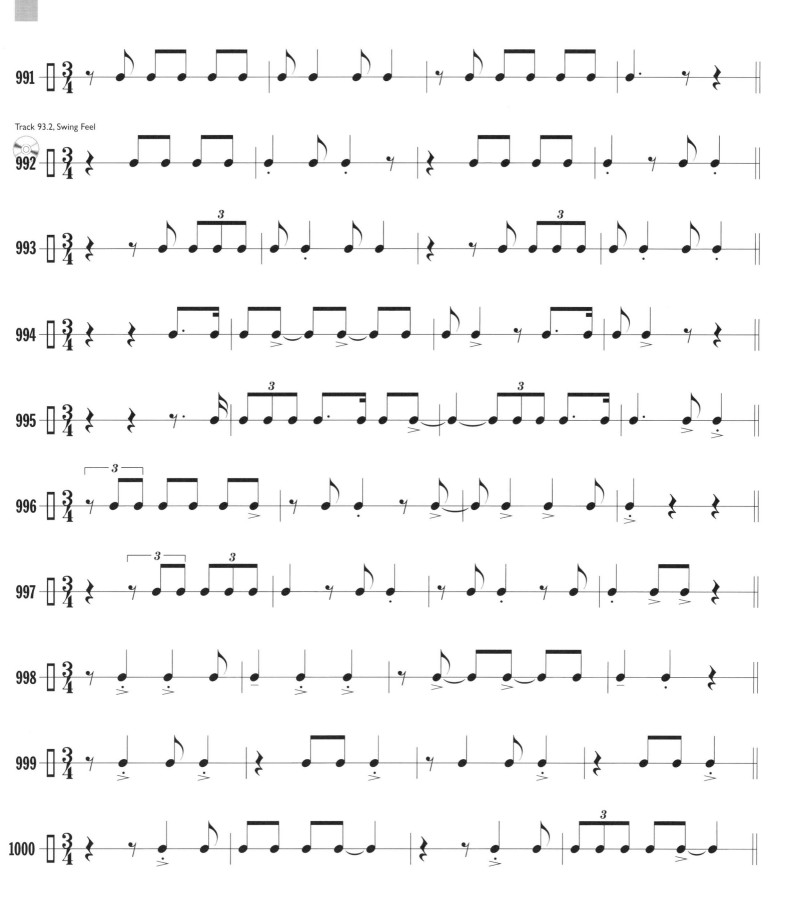

Ties Over the Barline

Exercises

1001–1010 Play these with a swing feel, and remember to mark the tied notes with a tap or click.

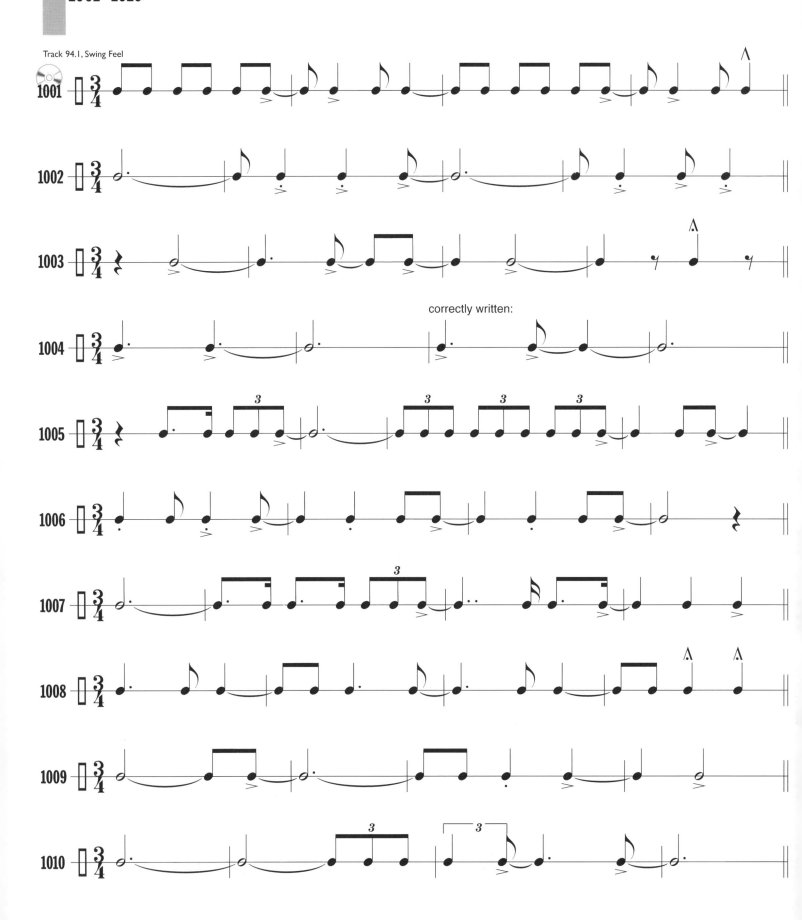

Staccato Notation

Exercises 1011–1020

Exercise 1017 introduces a new figure called the quadruplet, in which four notes are played in the space of three. In this case, four quarter notes are played in the space of three quarter notes, that is, in three beats. This means that the quarters have to be played faster than usual. How much faster can be shown by thinking 16th notes.

Thus, each quarter note is as long as three 16th notes. Another way of writing this figure can be seen in the last measure of Ex. 1017.

Track 94.2, Straight Feel

Track 94.3, Straight Feel

PART SIX : *Rhythms in Other Meters*

This section (pages 123–127) illustrates examples in 6/8, 3/8, 9/8 and 12/8. These rhythms are all based on a unit which contains three eighth notes. 3/8 has one unit per measure, 6/8 has two units per measure, 9/8 has three and 12/8 has four. At slow to moderate tempos, each eighth note is counted as one beat.

At faster tempos, each unit gets one beat:

Rhythms in 5/4 Time

Pages 128 and 129 illustrate the two most common ways of playing 5/4 time: as 3+2 or 2+3. As the only irregular meter illustrated in this book, 5/4 takes on extra importance because it illustrates the way irregular meters can be broken down into shorter, easier units. For example, 7/8 can be played as one measure of 3/8 followed by two beats from any 4/4 or 2/4 example. 10/4 could be played as one measure of 3/4 plus two measures of 2/4 plus one measure of 3/4. All irregular meters can be broken down into combinations of shorter measures you have already studied.

As you can see from the following examples, in which the basic rhythmic unit (the lower note of the time signature) is the eighth note, it's the way the beams connect the groups of eighth notes that is the key to proper interpretation. In each measure the first group of notes gets the primary accent; the following groups get a lighter accent.

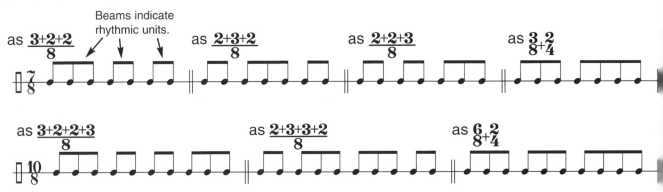

When the rhythmic unit is the quarter note or half note, the interpretation is harder to see, but can usually be figured out from the outline of the melody. Experienced composer/arrangers don't leave this to chance, but indicate the proper interpretation in the time signature, e.g., instead of a 7/4 time signature they might use $\frac{3+2+2}{4}$ or $\frac{2+2+3}{4}$ depending on which effect they want.

6/8 Time

Exercises
1021–1030

6/8 time is used for marches ("The Washington Post"), jigs ("The Irish Washerwoman," "Garryowen"), folk songs ("Molly Malone," "Home on the Range") and, occasionally, in modern stage band arrangements. When 6/8 is played at a slow to moderate tempo, count in six; each eighth note gets one beat. When the tempo is faster, count in two; each dotted quarter or group of three eighth notes gets one beat.

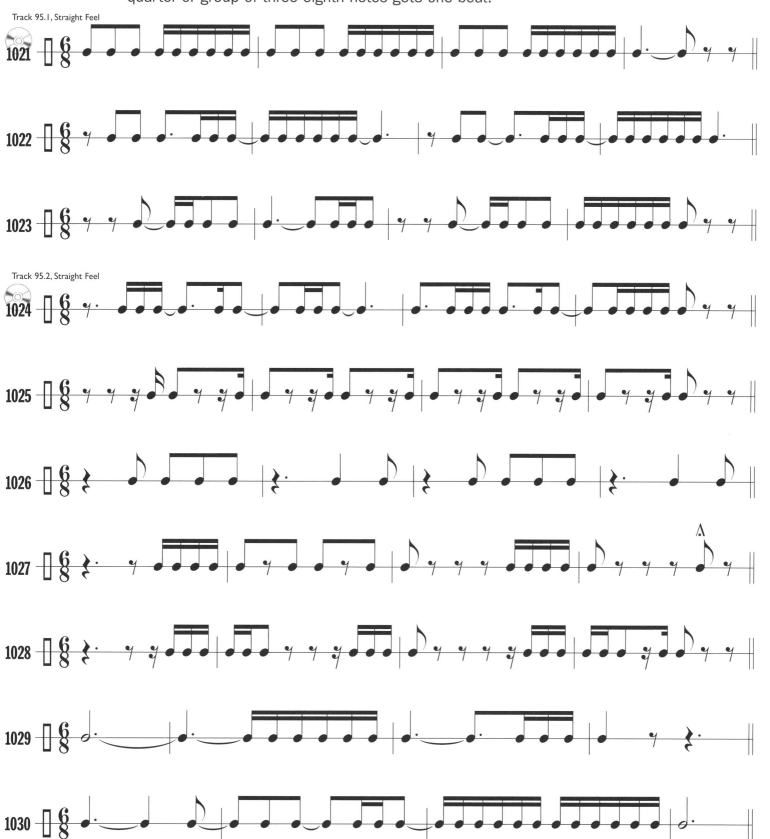

6/8 Time (cont.)

Exercises 1031–1040

Exercise 1037 introduces two new figures in 6/8 time:
The eighth notes in the second half of measures 1 and 3 are quadruplets. The number 4 means that the four notes are played in the time normally occupied by three eighth notes.

The figure in the second half of measure 2 is called a duplet. The number 2 means that the two quarter notes are played in the time normally occupied by three eighth notes. Confusingly, (as in Ex. 1039, measure 2) duplets are sometimes written as two *eighth* notes played in the space of three. Both figures are played the same.

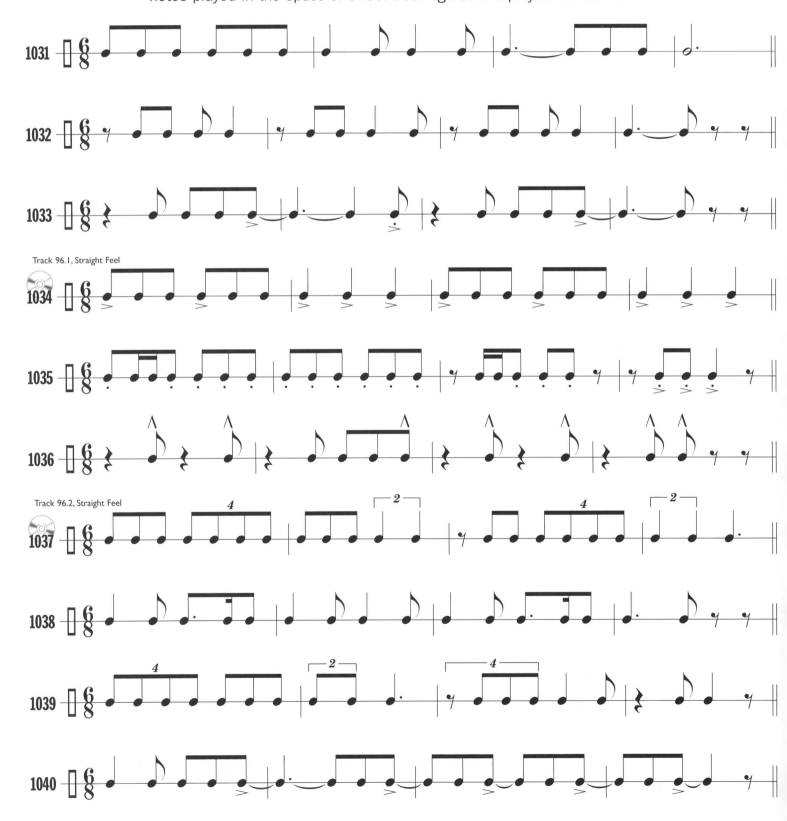

Track 96.1, Straight Feel

Track 96.2, Straight Feel

3/8 Time

Exercises
1041–1050

3/8 time is played exactly like a one half measure of 6/8. At slow to moderate tempos, count in three, one beat per eighth note. At faster tempos, count in one, with each dotted quarter getting one beat. 3/8 often appears in the midst of a 6/8 piece when half a measure is needed. It has also been used in folk music, e.g., "The Old Oaken Bucket."

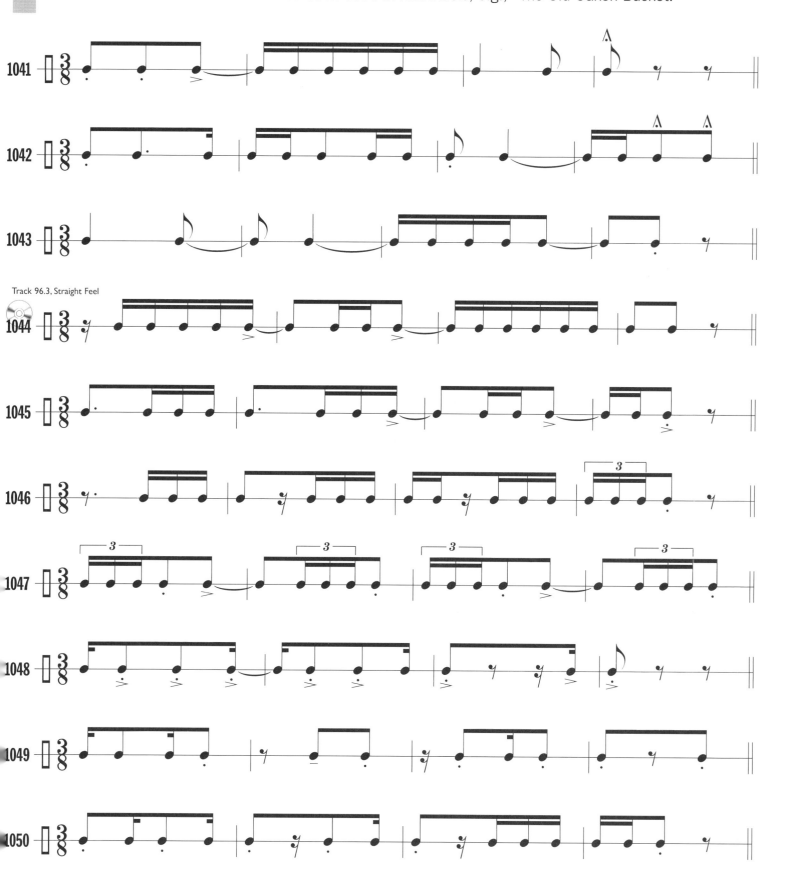

Track 96.3, Straight Feel

9/8 Time

Exercises
1051–1060 9/8 time is not often seen, but it has been used for some famous pieces of music, e.g., "The Ride of the Valkyries," "Send in the Clowns," "The Impossible Dream," and "Beautiful Dreamer." At slow to medium tempos, count in nine, with each eighth note getting one beat. At faster tempos, count in three, with each dotted quarter getting one beat.

Track 97.1, Straight Feel

Track 97.2, Straight Feel

12/8 Time

Exercises **1061–1070**

If it weren't for early rock and roll (e.g., Sonny and Cher's "I Got You, Babe"), 12/8 time would probably be unknown to today's pop musician. As usual in these types of meters, if the tempo is slow to moderate, play in twelve, with each eighth note getting one beat. At faster tempos, play in four, with each dotted quarter getting one beat. This meter is almost always played in four.

Track 97.3, Straight Feel

Track 97.4, Straight Feel

5/4 Time, Considered as 3+2

Exercises 1071–1080

5/4 time is an irregular meter that is usually played as one measure of 3/4 followed by a measure of 2/4 (as on this page), or as one measure of 2/4 followed by one measure of 3/4 (as on page 129). We know of only two well-known pieces in 5/4, Dave Brubeck's "Take Five," (which is based on the rhythm in Ex. 1076, measure 1) and the theme to "Mission Impossible," but since more and more modern arrangers and composers are using irregular meters, the serious player will want to master these rhythms as well.

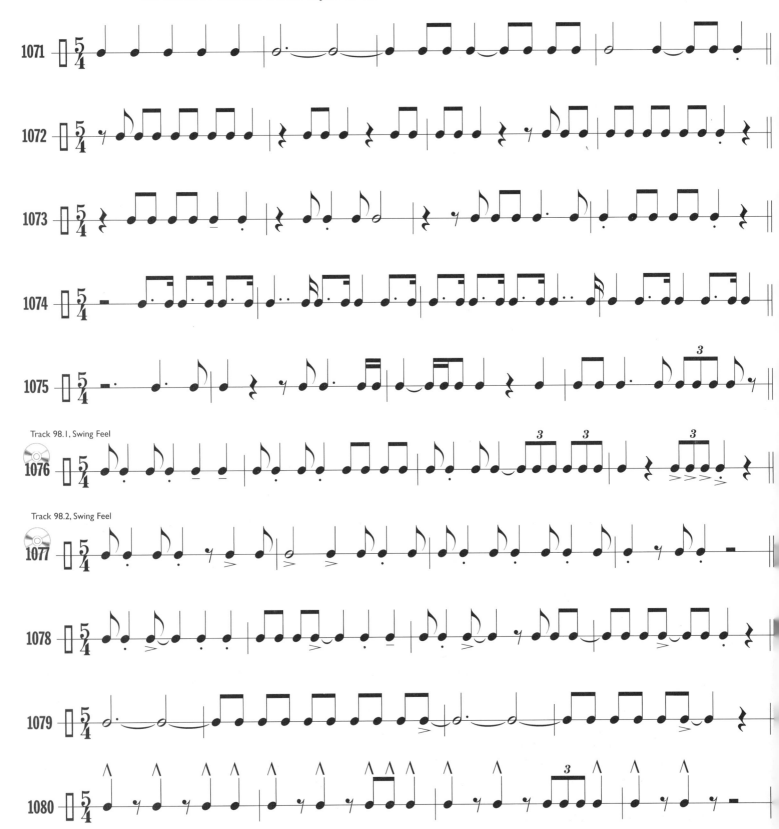